Karmapa

His Holiness the 17th Gyalwa

Karmapa

Urgyen Trinley Dorje

———

Ken Holmes

ISBN 0 9524555 4 4

British Library Cataloguing-in-Publication Data. A catalogue record for this book is available from the British Library.

Layout and setting by Altea Publishing
Printed by Redwood Books, Trowbridge, Wiltshire
Published in 1995 by Altea Publishing, Parkmount House, St Leonards Road,
Forres IV36 0DW, Scotland

Contents

Author's Acknowledgements

I would like to acknowledge my gratitude to all those who made this book possible. Special recognition must be given to Vita de Waal and Sandra Kramer, the publishers, for the initial inspiration as well as a constant, positive support; to my wife Katia for her invaluable advice and companionship throughout the task of authorship, and to all those whose camera lenses have captured the 16th and 17th Karmapas for the whole world to share, including Ward Holmes and the Tsurphu Foundation, Lea Wyler and Rokpa International, Bryan Miller, Michele Martin and Magda Wangyal. Thanks and gratitude also to Akong Tulku Rinpoche, the 12th Tai Situpa Rinpoche and Tsurphu Gyaltsap Rinpoche for use of photographs from their private collection. I am grateful to all others who offered their photos for use in this book, including Stephan Storm, Ani Ea, Rosi Findeisen and Chris Taylor.

Thanks also to Michele Martin for the poem on pages 33 and 34, which she translated under the guidance of Khenchen Thrangu Rinpoche in Baudhanath, Nepal, in April 1994.

Photo Credits

Colour section
Photos on pages 1, 4, 5, 6 (top), 7, 8, 10, 11, 12, 13 and 16 of colour section, © Ward Holmes/Tsurphu Foundation.
Photos on pages 2, 3, and 6 (bottom), from the private collection of Akong Tulku Rinpoche, the 12th Tai Situpa Rinpoche and Tsurphu Gyaltsap Rinpoche.
Photo on page 9 © Bryan Miller.
Photos on pages 14 & 15 © Magda Wangyal.

Black-and-white photos
Pages 19, 24, 25, 27, 45, 48, 50, 51, 53, 54, 66, 67, 79, 139, 140 and 141, from the private collection of Akong Tulku Rinpoche, the 12th Tai Situpa Rinpoche and Tsurphu Gyaltsap Rinpoche.
Pages 29, 33, 59, 61, 64, 70, 101, 102, 103, 104 and 142, © Ward Holmes/Tsurphu Foundation.
Page 52, permission for use given by Michele Martin.
Pages 57 and 63, © Michele Martin.
Page 71, © Magda Wangyal.
Page 82, © Rokpa International.

Dedication

Namo Guru Vajradhara

Might of compassion of all the buddhas and bodhisattvas,
inestimable in their numbers,
Incomparable perfect guide, lord and protector of beings,
the replete manifestation of Avalokitesvara,
You fully embody every aspect of the various classes of enlightened being,
and are the supreme victor, Karmapa Urgyen Drodul Trinley Dorje.
We pray that your sacred presence remain firmly with us forever.

[This heartfelt prayer was composed by the Tai Situpa at the request of His Holiness the Karmapa's European disciples]

Chapter One

Introduction

I would like to invite you to take an imaginary walk with me around the lake at Samye Ling, here in Scotland, on a bright summer's day. It is a pleasant and relaxing way to chat when asked for a little clarification on Buddhism. While admiring the water-lilies and listening to the chattering of chaffinches, one can take one's time explaining the traditional teachings and add the occasional example or metaphor, here and there, to help bring the whole thing to life. Our conversation will try to throw a little more light on this unique person, the 17th Gyalwa Karmapa, one of Tibet's most outstanding reincarnate lamas and the head of the Karma Kagyu tradition of Tibetan Buddhism.

Now that he has been discovered and enthroned, you may well meet him, in Tibet where he is at present or in India or the West, once it is possible for him to travel. Or perhaps you would like to read something about him. Although many newspaper and magazine articles on him have been published already, it has already become clear that a number of key points could benefit greatly from a little more reliable explanation — such as what really *is* a Karmapa and what is the Kagyu tradition that he embodies?

My contribution, as we pause to breathe in the pure Scottish air, is to pass on to you, as if you were talking with a friend 'on the inside', some of the information I have gathered from the Kagyu lineage's great lamas in the past few decades. I will paint the traditional picture of the Karmapas, trying to home in on those things very commonly misunderstood and not dwelling over-long on what is already well explained in other works. A quick glance at the contents will reveal that part of this book is about the extraordinary reincarnation story of the 17th Karmapa — how he was discovered and so forth — and part of it is about the teachings and lineage from which he is inseparable. And there are some striking photos.

This book came into being through the inspiration of Vita de Waal. In an exciting and fast-moving flow of events, like a crocus emerging from the earth, the spring of 1995 saw the concept of this work take form. Surprised at first to be the one asked to write a text on the Karmapas, I reflected a while and then agreed, feeling it might be a way of serving my late teacher, HH the 16th Karmapa, in his new incarnation, and of repaying in part his tremendous kindness towards myself, my wife Katia and many of our friends. I have written the book with a feeling of joy, yet great reservation.

The joy lay in the hope of being able to bring the reader a little closer to the Karmapa. My case is very typical: I probably represented one millionth of the late 16th Karmapa's world, perhaps even less if one is realistic, yet he has been the sun which transformed my entire life. In travelling at his side for some six months, through many different countries, I saw him awaken the fundamental goodness and spiritual potential in people, time after time. It was like being with the Buddha, 2,500 years ago in India — he embodied purity, grace, wisdom, kindness, strength, certainty.

Since that time, it has been the good fortune of Katia and I to have been charged by the 16th Karmapa with the study and translation of some of the main teaching works used in the Karma Kagyu tradition. While staying at his seat in Rumtek in 1980, Katia was also asked to translate two autobiographical texts, one recounting his own reincarnation tales, a thousand years previously, and another containing ten autobiographical stories from other ages, as told by the previous, 15th, Karmapa.

Work on these wonderful books — mainly under the guidance of two of the Kagyu tradition's main scholars, Khenchen Thrangu Rinpoche and Khenpo Tsultrim Gyamtso Rinpoche — gradually opened our eyes to, among other things, the uniquely exalted position the Karmapa holds. It is often the case that only knowledge of context makes one realise how precious something is. A rare emerald is no different from green glass to a baby. An average adult may know it to be valuable but only the gemologist or jeweller can fully appreciate the marvel he holds in his hands. To most Westerners, there is little to distinguish one red-robed or saffron-robed Buddhist from another. The better-informed may know something of the difference between monks, scholars, yogis and reincarnate lamas. But those who have some inkling of the vast range of possibilities of the human mind, as it journeys from here to enlightenment, will appreciate that among them all, those who have reached the end of that journey are exquisitely rare and that, even among these, the Karmapa shines like the brightest star in the heavens.

People's meetings with the Karmapa occur as the fruition of their actions in former lives. That is as it is and cannot be modified. However, at the time of meeting him, the way one relates to him and the preconceptions about him that one has developed in this life can make a big difference to what takes place. As the scriptures say,

> "... if one thinks of him as a Buddha, one will get a Buddha's blessing ... yet if one can only think of him as an ordinary man, then one can only receive what an ordinary man could give."

Therefore my hope is to introduce readers, especially those new to the subject, to some time-honoured teachings about the Karmapas, what they represent and the Buddhist context in which they are situated, according to the traditional instructions given by the main teachers of the Kagyu lineage and according to my own limited experience gleaned in a quarter century of practising, studying and then teaching Kagyu Buddhism to Westerners. But, as I mentioned, I also have great reservations: quite simply, they are those of a tiny flame asked to describe the sun.

◆ ◆ ◆

There would be little point in my repeating what can be found in the biographies of previous Karmapas and former patriarchs of the Kagyu lineage which are already published. It seems more appropriate to complement existing information with insights the reader might not find elsewhere. Lama Karma Thinley's excellent book *The Sixteen Karmapas of Tibet* and other fairly well-known publications take us one by one through the sixteen previous incarnations. As the Tai Situpa has so rightly said, it would require many years, if not decades, of research and consultation to establish reliable biographies of the Karmapas that will take one further than at present. The Karmapas travelled widely and had an influence which at times covered empires. Not only religious but also endless historical and political details need to be verified and cross-checked. For a 900-year period of history, this is a huge task, complicated by the disappearance of monastery and other records as a result of Tibet's turbulent history in the latter half of this century.

In sketching out the spiritual context in which Tibetan Buddhists view the Karmapa, I shall write from a Buddhist point of view, taking notions such as reincarnation and so forth as natural, yet explaining things wherever it might prove helpful. This is not a purely academic work of Western anthropology but, I hope, a living testimony from a contemporary Buddhist. I leave it to the readers to analyse what is said, according to their own philosophical leanings, taking or leaving whatever they feel it is right so to do.

◆ ◆ ◆

There is something extraordinarily pure, straightforward and simple about the Karmapa and his blessing. Those who have experienced it treat their every thought of the Karmapa with tremendous respect. In many mystic songs, they call the Karmapa 'he whose name is hard to pronounce'. This particular expression means a lot to me as it is hard for many of us to say his name or think of him without our hair standing slightly on end and feeling deeply, deeply moved by memories of his tremendous compassion. For that reason, I would not like to sully this book, which for me is a celebration of the Karmapa's purity, with excessive discussion of the polemic caused by the pitiable presentation of a counter-candidate to the 17th Karmapa's throne by a tiny faction of breakaway Kagyupas. Their pretence to power thrives on controversy and does all it can to stir it up. Urgyen Trinley Dorje has been welcomed as the one and true 17th Gyalwa Karmapa by almost the totality of Kagyu Buddhist lamas, by HH the Dalai Lama and by the heads of the two other main traditions of Tibetan Buddhism — HH Sakya Trichen

and HH Mingling Trichen. As we shall see, he was already chosen by his predecessor, the 16th Karmapa, whose very own prediction letter and mystic poems
revealed his clear knowledge of things to come. No more will be said of that small
cloud of darkness which hopes to blot out the sun.

Tibetan has a beautiful vocabulary of respectful terms to be used when speak-
ing with one's equals or superiors. Persons worthy of respect on account of their
spiritual accomplishment are often described by poetical periphrases that uplift
the mind. Tibetans might call the Karmapa 'The Wish-Fulfilling Gem, the One
Empowered by All the Enlightened Ones, the Karmapa' and for them just using
the word Karmapa sounds a little insufficient, even slightly disrespectful. On the
other hand, the reader, unused to this, may soon tire of such periphrases if they
are used every time the Karmapa is mentioned. Furthermore, a Tibetan biography would tend to enumerate all the facts of a master's life, in terms of studies
done and teachings given, whereas a Western mind finds this boring and loves
the spicier anecdotes — such as miracles. Respecting my Tibetan friends and Western readers, I have tried to strike a happy balance between these two and hope
you enjoy these words and images about a being who will certainly be one of the
great figures of the century about to commence.

Chapter Two

Tibet, Land of the New Karmapa's Birth

The land of Tibet, with its unique cultural and religious heritage, is almost as large as India. Yet it remains little known to the modern Western world, to which it is an anecdote — a mythical Shangri-la; the abode of the abominable snowman, or *yeti*. Some will only know it as a place where elaborately-clad lamas play deafening music on outlandish instruments. That is the image TV documentarists inevitably pick for its audiovisual impact. Whenever they visit Tibetans, they feel duty-bound to film the monks blowing the long horns (*ra-dong*), invariably shot by a cameraman prostrate on the carpet, wide-angling on the open end of the horn and then shifting focus to the pouting cheeks of the instrumentalist. Yet Tibet is so much more than these anecdotes and image-bytes.

Traditional Tibet made a striking contrast to our modern world. Before 1950 the radical differences between the two were apparent only to the few explorers and mystics who ventured into Tibet's isolated fastness. Since then it has struck many thousands of people now in close contact with Tibetan lamas following the latter's diaspora throughout the world. They left their homeland as a result of the progressive annexation of Tibet by China in the 1950s and the subsequent total suppression of its religion up to and during the Cultural Revolution.

What contrast? That between spiritual and material advancement. Tibet's colourfully vivid land of vibrant earth and sky was mostly peopled by unwashed nomads living an almost Bronze Age life in hide tents under extremes of climate one would expect on the 'roof of the world', or else by farmers and villagers living in a neo-feudal society, many aspects of which we would associate with the Middle Ages. But in amongst these rude physical conditions there also existed, in monasteries and hermitages, one of the finest flowers of human thought and contemplation: refined, subtle, codified by centuries of intellectual reflection and masterly meditation, and centred in a vision of compassionate love for all life and of living in harmony with the natural world and the elements upon which life itself depends. This vision of life influenced everything in Tibet and coloured every Tibetan's daily round. Within the seemingly primitive, there existed one of humankind's most advanced and gentlest approaches to existence.

This is so different to our seemingly advanced, highly technological, daily-cleaned modern world in which, for all its material advantages, the life-glow of inner wisdom, natural happiness, care for others and care for nature seem to diminish decade by decade. Within 'advanced' 20th-century society, one often encounters the violent and primitive. I do not mean to imply that the Tibetans are all right and the modern world all wrong. We simply all have a lot to learn from each other when it comes to working out what 'progress' really signifies.

The Tibetan heritage is one of the many messengers of light to have entered the global forum in recent times. Let us hope that it may be a factor of help in the shaping of a better future for generations to come.

The following is some background information which may help readers sketch an image of Tibet in their imagination. It is not only the land which cradled the Kagyu Buddhist tradition, of which the Gyalwa Karmapa is the head, but also the land in which he has now reincarnated, choosing birth among its nomads. It is too early to tell why this was the case. Yet it must certainly be of importance when one considers that, for the first time in his lineage's history, it would have been feasible for him to have taken birth in the West, in India or in the Far East, following the establishment of Kagyu Buddhism throughout the world during the 70s and 80s by his previous (16th) incarnation and the main lamas of his school. Yet he chose Tibet.

Geography

It may help those a little uncertain in their Asian geography to locate Tibet roughly by picturing it sitting atop India, to the left of China, and beneath the former Soviet Union. Although the modern Autonomous Region of Tibet in China bears the Tibetan name, it is but part of the natural geographical and linguistic zone which forms Tibet proper. The remaining parts have been absorbed into the Chinese provinces of Xinjiang, Quinghai, Sichuan and Yunnan since the 1960s.

To be more precise, Tibet is the world's highest land mass, covering some 3.8 million square kilometres (1.5 m square miles), i.e. more than seven times the size of France or Texas. Most of this is a plateau, the valleys of which start higher than Mont Blanc or Mt Whitney, while its own famous peaks, soaring up to 8,000 metres (24,000 feet), are the highest in the world. Its natural borders are formed by the Himalayas to the south, the Taklamakan desert to the west and north-west, the alpine desert, steppe and Kunlun mountains to the north and the natural fall-off of the plateau in the east, towards Chengdu in China.

Tibetans live mainly along the southern belt and in the eastern region of Tibet, in the lower valleys at altitudes of 3-4,000 metres, with passes between valleys often at 5,000 metres. Although this high altitude gives an immediate impression of great cold and Tibet is famous as 'the Land of Snows', one must also bear in mind that it is on the same latitudes as Algeria.

The immense highland region known as the Northern Plain (*byang.thang*, pronounced *chang tang*), which accounts for more than half of Tibet, is an arid, cold, wind-blasted semi-desert with thousands of salt-lakes and salt-flats, little conducive to habitation yet nevertheless home to more than half a million Tibetan nomads. Tibet is almost the only remaining example of a country dependent upon nomadic pastoralism — a way of life once widespread throughout the world.

The dominant feature of the inhabited parts of Tibet is its rivers, making it a

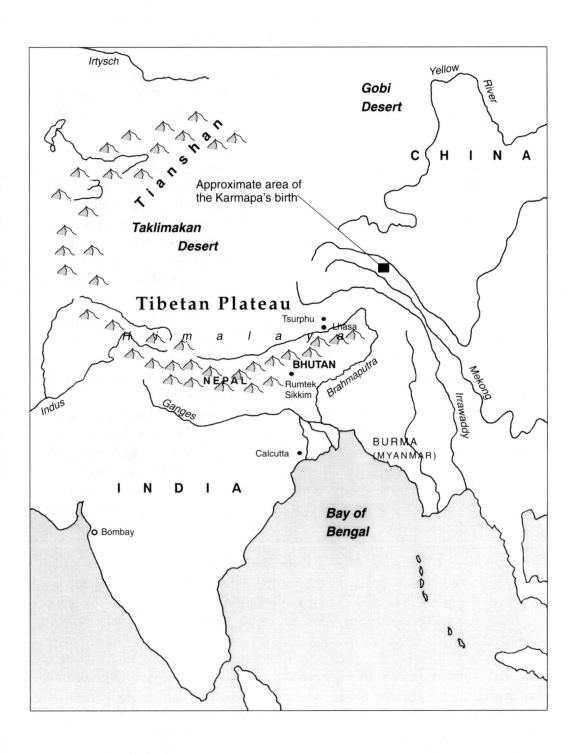

land of alternating valleys and mountain ranges, each having their particular characteristics and local climate. Many great rivers rise in Tibet: the Huang Ho (Yellow River), the Yangtze, the Mekong, the Salween, the Indus and the Brahmaputra, to name a few. It is interesting to note, from an ecological as well as from an earth-energy point of view, that so much of Asia's water supply comes from the Tibetan highlands. Those who have enjoyed hikes up mountains and the pleasure of crystal clear mountain streams will understand the very special quality of waters that originate in the closest places on earth to the heavens, high above the dense, polluted atmosphere of the lowlands. This is even more true of Tibet, the roof of the world, upon whose melting snows and glaciers so much of Asian life depends. It now seems certain that the recent Ice Ages, which affected the whole Northern Hemisphere, were caused by the rise of the Tibetan plateau, the subsequent monsoon cycles so created and the monsoon-sodden wet rocks of the new Himalayas leeching out carbon dioxide from the atmosphere (the opposite of the greenhouse effect). One should never underestimate the geographical importance of Tibet and always bear in mind the fact that hundreds of millions of people in India and China will be affected by any radical changes in its ecology.

Climate

The Northern Plain is a windy, dusty area exposed to violent solar radiation. Little rain or snow falls, yet there are innumerable rivers and salt lakes, fed by melting glaciers. Winters are long and extremely cold (down to -35°C) and summers see hot days (30°C) yet cold nights (-15°C). Southern Tibet has a less violent climate, warmer and damper than the Northern Plain, making it more inhabitable. Most rain there falls in the summer, although this is too far north for monsoon rains. Snow falls in early autumn, early winter and late spring. The south-west is dry and cold; mainly alpine steppes. The more fertile central southern area has lower valleys of shrubby steppe becoming more forested as one moves east, where it is warmer and damper.

The rich eastern area of Tibet is a complex terrain of mountain ranges, each with its specific climate. Amdo, to the north-east, is a vast land of steppe and pasture. As one moves south, to Khams, where the rainfall is higher, the steppe becomes forested and shrubby, while to the far south-east the climate becomes sub-tropical.

High altitude makes the ever-present sun (3,400 hours of sunlight per year, i.e. almost ten hours per day) extremely strong all over Tibet, even though the temperature in the shade may not be that high. Tibetans have learnt to live with the cold by wearing thick skin clothing with the fur turned inwards and by imbibing endless cups of hot salted butter tea to restore the calories they lose. They have learnt to live with the sun, protecting their faces with daubed-on pastes and their heads with an amazing variety of hats.

Peoples

Archaeological discoveries of this century are revealing more and more about the humans who have inhabited Tibet over the millennia. Microlithic tools found in central Tibet, belonging to the Old Stone Age, could originate from any period up to 10,000 years ago. At some time since then nomadic pastoralism was introduced from south-east Asia. Farming villages and ancient dwellings found in Khams in the east and also in the north-east show early 'modern human' presence there, in villages, some 5,000 years ago. Our picture of the history of Tibet in relatively recent times, i.e. up to some 1,500 years ago, is still sketchy and a subject of much research at present, with various pieces of the jigsaw being contributed by archaeology, Tibet's own legends and historical research from neighbouring lands.

The people themselves show traces of many different ethnic groups, as one would imagine from a land plumb in the heart of Asia and through the trade routes in contact with Chinese, Mongol, Indian and Middle Eastern influences. However, seen from a distance there are two distinct types: those of a shorter, Mongol stock and the others. The strong sunlight gives them all dark skins and puts a beautiful apple-red glow on the cheeks of their moon-faced ladies. Once married, these latter wear distinctive rainbow aprons and love turquoise, coral, amber and mother-of-pearl adornments. The men wear long-sleeved, dark-coloured voluminous coats, known as *chupa*, and bear themselves with silent dignity. As one might expect of people living in such a climate and isolation, the Tibetans are resourceful, single-minded and hospitable.

The name Tibet has been adopted by Westerners from the word used for that land by Moslem authors since the 9th century, 'Tubbat', 'Tüpüt' or 'Tibbat'. This was picked up by European travellers of the Middle Ages, such as Plan de Carpin, Marco Polo and Francesco della Penna. Tibetans themselves called their land 'Bod', pronounced *Bö*, which, according to their own records, was its name even in the times of the Buddha. Some say that the Chinese originally knew it as *fan*, which means Barbary, but on the advice of a Tibetan ambassador diplomatically changed it to *T'ou-fan* which incorporates *T'ou-fa*, their name for Turco-Mongols. *T'ou-fa* probably started out as Tuppat, the Islamic word mentioned above.

Tibetans speak a language of the Tibeto-Burmese group, a family of tongues distinct from the Indo-European and Chinese languages. It is not impossible, according to linguistic evidence, that an original Proto-Tibeto-Burmese people centred somewhere around present-day northern Burma (Myanmar) and Yunnan gradually spread west through Tibet and south into Burma and neighbouring areas.

Livelihood

There have been four major ways of life in Tibet: farming, nomadic animal husbandry, trading and religion. The first two of these are directly related to the climate and geography of local regions. In the lower and more lush valleys it is possible to work the earth and to grow a variety of crops, principally cereals such as barley, wheat, millet, rice and maize, and also peas and potatoes. In the most temperate regions, apples, oranges, pears and even apricots and bananas grow. However, the most widespread crops are climate-resistant barleys and wheats. Barley grains, roasted and ground, make the famous Tibetan *tsampa* flour, which is kneaded with tea and butter as a staple diet, accompanied by dried or cooked meat.

In areas where the land and climate make arable agriculture impossible, nomads rely upon the vast expanses of grasslands to support them, moving from camp to camp with their herds of sheep, yaks and yak-cattle hybrids according to the humours of the four seasons. They live almost exclusively on meat and dairy products, accompanied by *tsampa* and other grains. Vegetables and fruit have been little eaten, if at all, in Tibet, not only because of their rarity but also because they often take more calories to digest than they later give back to the body. In a land of cold where thick sheepskin clothing is the order of the day, calories are a vital consideration.

The farming and nomadic communities in Tibet have always depended upon each other; the farmers on nomads for their meat produce and the nomads on farmers for their grains. With so few people living in such a vast and disparate space, trading was of vital importance. Those prepared to face the dangers and hardships of long journeys were able to support themselves and their families by their wit in negotiation, plying between nomads, farmers, craftspeople and the monasteries, whose economic importance was not negligible.

Although in the long term the monks and nuns depended upon farmers, nomads and traders for their sustenance, they need to be mentioned for their sheer numbers and their omnipresence in Tibetan life. Some say that up to 25% of the male population were monks. This is not surprising, considering that there were many thousands of monasteries, nunneries and hermitages in Tibet and that the very largest were home to several thousand persons.

Estimates of the pre-1959 Tibetan population vary from 4.5 to 6 million. This gave a population density of one person per two square kilometres, or in other words four or five hundred times as much space per person as a British or American citizen enjoys. Present estimates put the population somewhere around 15 million, the sharp rise being due to the influx of Chinese soldiers and civilians.

The Tibetan people and their way of life remained little changed until the middle of this century. It is tempting still to think of Tibet in terms of how it was, especially when trying to understand its religion and its great religious figures, such as the Karmapas. Nevertheless, whatever our personal feelings may be, we must acknowledge that, to all intents and purposes, Tibet has been part of China for almost forty years now — and much has changed. It is not within the scope of this book to depict or comment upon those changes; simply to sketch a traditional picture of a land dear to many of our hearts, that has safeguarded a remarkable religion and produced some of the most extraordinary minds we have ever encountered.

'Jowo Rinpoche', the statue of Sakyamuni housed in the Jokhang temple, before which the 17th Karmapa's naming and hair-cutting ceremonies took place (see Chapter 6).

Religion

Although Tibet is famous now for its Buddhism, one must mention the pre-Buddhist Bön religion, which has survived alongside Buddhism in Tibet. As some elements of Buddhist belief are explained in other chapters of this book, all that will be said about it here is that it is a way of living based upon a quest for inner peace and world peace, respect for others, dedication to the happiness not only of humankind but also of the animal kingdom and any form of sentient life, generosity, self-control and a deep love of knowledge. It does not believe in God as a creator but does believe in a powerful, pure and compassionate essence common to each and every being and known as *buddha nature*.

The Bön religion was originally a form of shamanism. It has been greatly modified over the centuries, to keep pace with Buddhism, many of the ideas and forms of which have been integrated into it, after considerable adaptation. One speaks generally of white Bön and black Bön, the former being the version which has modelled itself around Buddhism and the latter being the one which has stayed close to its shamanistic roots.

The 7th-century Tibetan king Söntsen Gampo (*sron.btsan.sgam.po*) made major efforts to establish Buddhism in Tibet, which traditionally followed Bön, and to bring his country out of its isolation. He built up Tibet's military strength to a point where the monarchs of neighbouring countries thought it wise to enter into treaty with him. First the Nepalese king Amsuvarman and later the Chinese emperor T'aitsung offered their royal princesses to him in marriage. These maidens, Bhrukuti and Wen-Ch'eng, brought magnificent Buddhist statues of Aksobhya, Maitreya and Sakyamuni to Tibet with them as wedding gifts. Söntsen Gampo introduced the ten basic moral laws of Buddhism into Tibet's legal code and sent his brilliant scholar Thonmi Sambhota to India to study its linguistics in order to establish a Tibetan alphabet and written language with a grammar which would suit the translation of Buddhist texts. He also constructed a residence on the site which was later to become the 11-storey Potala palace and he built the Ramoche and Jokhang temples to house the statues brought by his queens. It was before the statue of Sakyamuni in the Jokhang temple that the 17th Karmapa received the Buddhist hair-cutting and naming ceremony.

However, Buddhism was unable to implant itself in Tibet due to the deep-rootedness of the Bön religion and it was to take three more difficult centuries for Buddhism to become the true religion of the Tibetan people. Söntsen Gampo's own achievements did not have a widespread effect and it was only with his fifth descendant, Trisong Detsen (*khri.srong.lde.btsan*), in the 8th century, that a real first conversion of Tibet occurred.

Of the many traditions, lineages and sub-sects of Buddhism to have existed in Tibet, five main schools predominated. The oldest is the Nyingma (ancient) tradition, founded during that 8th-century conversion. This proved more successful than the previous attempt, due to the powerful combination of King Trisong Detsen's royal patronage, the Indian scholar Santaraksita's erudition and, above all, the spiritual might of Guru Rinpoche. However, this widespread implantation of Buddhism was all but wiped out by the ravages of a violently anti-Buddhist king called 'Ox-horns' (*glang.dar.ma*), reputed to have horns on his head.

The 11th century saw a powerful wave of restorative activity, with much intercourse between Tibet and India, and this gradually led to the establishment of the other four schools. They are collectively known as the *gsar.ma* (new) traditions.

The great Indian scholar Atisa's travels in Tibet gave rise to the purist (*kha.dam.pa*) movement which was to become the main source of the *Gelugpa* tradition, founded by Tsong Khapa in the 14th century and famous for its Dalai Lamas. Marpa the Translator, a contemporary and friend of Atisa, brought the *Marpa Kagyu* tradition to Tibet and Chungpo Naljor brought the *Shangpa Kagyu*.

At about that same time the *Sakya* tradition too was founded.

The history of spiritual and temporal power in Tibet since then is quite complex. Many people assume that the Dalai Lamas have always been the kings of all the Tibetan plateau and that they held religious sway over all Tibet. In fact, Tibet was a series of independent kingdoms and the Dalai Lama's influence was mainly felt in Central Tibet, the stronghold of his Gelugpa tradition which, as we have seen, is only a few centuries old. The other three traditions each had their leaders, as did the sub-branches of those traditions, but in general Tibetans spoke of the 'four great lamas of Tibet' (*bod.bla.chen.bzhi*):

The Karmapa — head of the Karma Kamtsang and most famous lama of the Kagyu traditions,

Sakya Trichen — head of the Sakya tradition, a leadership held in rotation by two reincarnating lamas,

Mindroling Tulku — head of the Nyingma tradition and

Gaden Tripa — the official, elected head of the Gelugpa tradition, of which the Dalai Lama is the reincarnate figurehead, as well as being a temporal monarch.

Tibetan medicine and environment

The Tibetan people have always lived in close harmony with their unique habitat. The isolation of their encampments and villages made it essential for them to know the healing qualities of the plants, minerals and animal products that made up their everyday world. Over the centuries Tibetan kings and scholars invited physicians from other lands and integrated into this natural knowledge the skills of Ayurvedic medicine from India and those of Chinese medicine, with its detailed insight into the interplay of the elements. With this was combined the Buddhist understanding of how mind and matter interact and how the human body is in resonance with the universe around it. Altogether, these produced one of the most sophisticated and holistic medical sciences in existence, rooted in millennia of practical experience, which it is now vital to preserve for future generations, not just of Tibetans but of all humankind.

Tibet is home to a vast range of herbs and plants, more than two thousand of which are used medicinally. Although more than one thousand varieties of tree were native to Tibet, the land has suffered severe deforestation in recent years, with all its consequent problems. Sadly, the fauna, comprising some two hundred species of mammal and almost six hundred species of bird, has greatly diminished in recent decades too and now includes many of the world's endangered species, such as the snow leopard. In particular, the great herds of wild mammals have dramatically declined, reminiscent of the loss of the buffalo herds on the American prairies. The land itself is one of the most beautiful on Earth, with a quality of light and colour, spaciousness and natural majesty that suit it well as one of the great repositories of our world's spirituality.

Chapter Three

The 16th Gyalwa Karmapa

The past thirty years have brought Tibetan Buddhism to the world at large. It is as though the tremendous wave of inspiration that carried the Buddha's teachings from India to Tibet in the 11th century surged back off that land's rocks and mountains, nine hundred years later, onto the entire planet. What brought this about entailed, in fact, the gravest of horrors for the Tibetan people: the total destruction of their Buddhism by the events leading up to China's 'cultural revolution'. Yet, through it, teachings safeguarded behind the Himalayan wall for almost a millennium have emerged to contribute to humankind's assets at a most critical point in its history. It has been a cruelly expensive yet exquisitely beautiful gift from Tibet to the world.

Although the first televised images of the Dalai Lama, in the early '60s, seem to have made a great impression on many people at the time, the general response to the Tibetan refugee lamas was initially small. But it grew, slowly at first and then almost exponentially. Within two decades, hundreds of Tibetan Buddhist centres became established in Europe, America, the Far East and, interestingly, India and Nepal, the lands in which Buddhism originated. This growth occurred through spontaneous interest, without any proselytising, which is against Buddhist ethics. The early key figures on the Tibetan side of this meeting of cultures were HH the Dalai Lama, HH the 16th Karmapa, HH Sakya Trizin, Kalu Rinpoche, Dudjom Rinpoche, Dilgo Khyentse Rinpoche, Trungpa Rinpoche, Akong Rinpoche and many others. Within the Kagyu tradition, the responsibility for providing inspiration and guidance during those vital years of first contact fell upon the 16th Karmapa.

The 16th Gyalwa Karmapa, Rangjung Rikpe Dorje, was born in the kingdom of De-ge, in eastern Tibet, in 1923, as the son of a noble family called A-toop. Having received predictions that she would bear a great bodhisattva son, his mother had gone to stay in a holy cave, once used by Guru Rinpoche, where she waited to give birth. It is said that, at one point at the very end of the pregnancy, the future Karmapa disappeared entirely from his mother's womb for a whole day. He was to do many such things in his life which would confound materialists and doctors, as witnessed by physicians in the Chicago hospital where he eventually died. On the day of his birth, his mother returned to normal pregnancy size and soon gave birth to him. Those present heard him say to his mother that he would be leaving. Water in offering bowls there turned to milk. Realising that she had indeed given birth to a great bodhisattva, his mother pretended to have had a daughter, in order to protect the child through secrecy.

The 11th Tai Situpa, one of the most eminent lamas of the Kagyu tradition,

HH the 16th Gyalwa Karmapa (left) with his teacher, the 11th Tai Situpa.

soon recognised the A-toop child as being the new Gyalwa Karmapa and sought official approval from HH the Dalai Lama. The details of the birth coincided properly with those of a prediction letter entrusted by the 15th Karmapa to his attendant[1]. Meanwhile, the child received his first ordination and bodhisattva vows from the Tai Situpa and from Palpung Kongtrul Rinpoche — his predecessor's two foremost disciples. Eventually, the Dalai Lama gave his acknowledgement. The boy was eight years old and still residing in the De-ge kingdom, where he received the Vajra Crown and ceremonial robes of the Karmapa, brought to him from Tsurphu. He visited Palpung monastery, stopping to bless the famous De-ge monastic printing works on the way, and was enthroned there as the 16th Karmapa, Rangjung Rikpe Dorje, by Palpung's chief abbot, the Tai Situpa, who shortly afterwards accompanied him on the long journey to the seat of the Karmapas at Tsurphu, close to Lhasa in central Tibet, where the new incarnation was greeted by Gyaltsab Rinpoche, Palpung Kongtrul and Pawo Rinpoche.

Soon after his arrival, the Karmapa was received by the 13th Dalai Lama, who performed the 'hair-cutting' ceremony. While so doing, the Dalai Lama had a vision of the celestial bodhisattva crown on the Karmapa's head. After this ceremony, the Karmapa was given a second enthronement, at Tsurphu, by the Tai Situpa and the head of the Drukpa Kagyu school. He then studied for some years under Gongkar Rinpoche, an extremely erudite scholar who had mastered the

[1]For a fuller account of this, see Chapter 5, *Finding the New Karmapa*

entire *tripitaka* and who recorded several stories of former lives told to him by the young Karmapa. It was a great loss that these stories remained with him in Tibet at the time of the troubles. He never escaped and the records were lost.

The Karmapa continued his studies within the Kagyu tradition by returning to Palpung and there receiving two comprehensive series of empowerments and teachings from the Tai Situpa: the 'Treasury of Kagyu Vajrayana Teachings' and the 'Treasury of Sacred Instructions'. Around this time, while visiting Pangpook monastery, it is said that not only did both the Gyalwa Karmapa and the Tai Situpa leave footprints in the rocks, but so also did the Karmapa's horse and dog! Some time later, the Karmapa, still based at Palpung, received a full transmission of the teachings of the Sakya tradition.

The 18-year-old Karmapa returned to Tsurphu. From 1941 to 1944 he spent much time in retreat, while in the world at large World War II was being fought to its conclusion. Tsurphu monastery was extended during this period. The Karmapa then went on pilgrimage to Samye, to Lodrak in the south of Tibet where Marpa had first introduced the Kagyu teachings, and then on to Bhutan. In 1945 the Tai Situpa gave him full ordination vows (*bhikkhu*) and further comprehensive Kagyu teachings on the giving of empowerments. He also received from the great Nyingma master Urgyen Rinpoche complete transmission of the Nyingma teachings of Terton Chojur Lingpa, who had made important predictions about the lives of the Karmapas, up to the twenty-first.

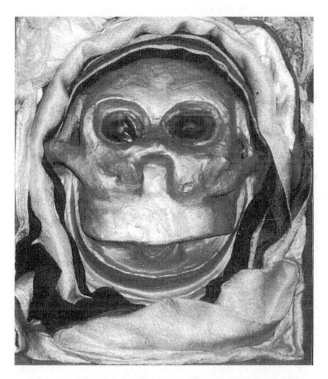

The mummified head of Santiraksita, first Abbot of Samye

In 1947 he travelled to India, Nepal and Sikkim, which was an independent kingdom at the time but is now part of India. His pilgrimage included the major places of the Buddha's life: Lumbini, just inside Nepal, where the Buddha was born, Benares (Varanasi) where he first taught and Bodh Gaya, the place of his enlightenment. Upon his return to Tsurphu in 1948, he received the final transmissions of the Kagyu teachings from two gurus: Palpung Kongtrul and the 11th Tai Situpa, who was now very advanced in years . By this time his training was complete, not only in the Kagyu but also the Sakya and Nyingma traditions. Indeed, in 1953, he was to pass on the Chojur Lingpa teachings to Mindroling Rinpoche, head of the Nyingma tradition and one of Tibet's 'four great lamas'.

By the 1950s the turbulence that was to result in the annexation of Tibet by China was already stirring. In 1954 the Karmapa, the young Dalai Lama and other leading representatives of Tibetan Buddhism went to Peking in response to an invitation from the Chinese government. While there, the Karmapa had a vision of the reincarnation of his teacher, the Tai Situpa, who had passed away in 1952, and sent instructions to the Tai Situ's monastery at Palpung. The child was found, exactly according to his instructions, and he enthroned him at the Palpung seat on his return journey from Peking to Tsurphu. During his stopover in eastern Tibet, several hundred Kagyu reincarnate lamas gathered around him and, obviously aware of the troubles in store, he transmitted to them many teachings and empowerments, as well as giving extensive ordinations. During this time, he gave the most secret and powerful protector empowerments. These are given only once in a lifetime and to only thirteen lamas. Of the hundreds of tulkus present, some relatively unknown ones, such as Akong Tulku of Drolma Lhakang, were summoned secretly to be part of the thirteen. It is very interesting that these were all later to play key roles in establishing the buddhadharma in the world at large.

The Karmapa returned to eastern Tibet in 1955, to act as a peacemaker between the local Tibetans and the Chinese military, brokering a five-year peace accord. He then travelled on to Sikkim and from there continued on pilgrimage. Buddhists worldwide had agreed to lay aside their differences over the dates of the Buddha's life and to celebrate the 2,500th anniversary of Buddhism in 1956. This was based upon the date marked on the historic Asoka stone pillar, which has Lord Buddha's passing from this world as (the equivalent of) 544 BCE. It was not only the celebration of a round number of years but also that of the beginning of the 6th era, as the Buddha had predicted the evolution of his teaching as taking place in ten 500-year periods. HH the Dalai Lama, HH the Karmapa and HH the Panchen Lama visited India to participate in the anniversary at the invitation of the Indian Mahabodhi Society. The Karmapa and his party revisited the holy sites of India as pilgrims. During this visit to India and Sikkim, he renewed his acquaintance with his disciples Tashi Namgyal, the maharaja of Sikkim, and Azhi Wangmo, the Bhutanese princess and devoted Buddhist practitioner. The maharaja invited him to visit Rumtek, a small monastery in Sikkim which the 9th Gyalwa

HH the 16th Karmapa in the late 1950s

Karmapa had founded at the end of the 16th century. His Holiness was unable to accept his invitation at that time but said that he would go there in the future, when it would be needed.

The next few years were to prove critical. His Holiness recognised several important new reincarnations, including Gyaltsab[2] Rinpoche, Palpung Jamgon Kongtrul and Drongsar Chentse, and Tsurphu became the refuge of Kagyu tulkus fleeing the violence that had again erupted in eastern Tibet between its people and the Chinese forces. These included Palpung's great yogi, Kalu Rinpoche, and the young Tai Situ, Tralek and Sangye Nyenpa tulkus. These young reincarnations were to be the future heart of the Kagyu lineage and His Holiness nurtured them with great care. Some he sent to safety fairly early on, such as the Tai Situpa and Sangye Nyenpa, who were accompanied by Kalu Rinpoche to Bhutan. Foreseeing the inevitable horrors that were to befall Buddhism in Tibet, the 16th Karmapa informed the Dalai Lama, in the spring of 1959, of his intention of leaving his homeland in order to preserve the greatest 'wealths' of his lineage: the clear young minds of its incarnate lamas and any portable spiritual treasures and

---

[1] *Gyaltsab* means regent. The Gyaltsabpa is the Karmapa's regent at Tsurphu monastery during his absence and in interregna. He is therefore sometimes known as Tsurphu Gyaltsab Rinpoche and is also known as the Goshir Gyaltsabpa.

relics. He led a party of some 150 tulkus, monks and laypeople on a relatively easy escape journey to Bhutan. It took three weeks on foot.

It must have been a moving and awe-inspiring journey for his party. Accompanied by the leader they loved so dearly, they first passed through the southern area of Lodrak, where Marpa and Milarepa had created the history of their tradition and where still stood the nine-storey tower built single-handedly by Milarepa almost nine hundred years previously in back-breaking conditions as a trial of faith in his master. When they were approaching the 6,000-metre pass which marks the border between Bhutan and Tibet, most people wanted to stop and rest, yet His Holiness urged them on, saying that it was vital to cross that very day. They did so and that same night heavy snows fell blocking off the Chinese pursuers close behind them. The Karmapa's perspicacity saved them from certain capture, as they had been unaware of being followed. In Bhutan they were warmly received by the princess, now a nun, and the Tai Situpa and Kalu Rinpoche came to join the Karmapa.

The Karmapa himself continued on to Sikkim, where he was again warmly received by the royal family and formally invited to establish his new seat. Of the several sites proposed, he decided it best to settle at Rumtek — the monastery built by the 9th Karmapa but now almost in ruins. He made the prophetic statement that he hoped one day to return to Tibet but that Rumtek could be his seat outside of Tibet. The generosity of the Sikkimese royal family and, a little later, of the Indian government, following the Karmapa's meeting with Pandit Nehru, funded most of the construction of the new Rumtek. The Indian government donated 1.4 million rupees.

After the initial turmoil of flight, a new reality was starting to take shape for Tibetans in India and the Himalayan kingdoms, living in refugee camps such as the one at Baxa. Some of the first contacts were made with sympathetic Westerners, including the now famous Freda Bedi, and an understanding of the world at large began to form. The main task in the Karmapa's hands were to ensure the continuity of his lineage through the education of the young tulkus in his charge and the transmission to them of the many teachings and techniques of the Kagyu tradition, and to establish the temples and retreat centres necessary to facilitate this. Yet, in another way, he simply continued to do what Karmapas have always done. The 16th Karmapa sometimes shocked his followers, who saw him as a living Buddha and one of the most important people in Asia, by declaring in total sincerity, "I am simply a monk." Unattached to any country, any people or any thing — a friend and example for everyone — it was his duty as a monk to give teachings and nurture the dharma wherever he might be. This also explains the example he set by supervising construction work at Tsurphu right up to the imminent arrival of the Chinese. He doubtless knew what was to come and some may wonder why he bothered. He was pointing to the sacred duty of doing all one can, every day, in a positive way. Thus his followers had made the good karma

Rumtek monastery in Sikkim

of building temples for absolutely as long as it was possible so to do and that good karma would be their best companion in times to come.

In 1964, following a successful petition for reinstatement made to HH the Dalai Lama by the unofficial Shamar incarnation, the latter was enthroned by HH the Gyalwa Karmapa as the 11th Shamarpa. His reincarnation had also been born into the A-toop family and the young boy had been at Tsurphu and fled Tibet with the Karmapa but official recognition had been impossible in Tibet itself as Shamarpa incarnations had been banned by edict of the central Tibetan government from the late 18th century onwards, following accusations of war-mongering.

By 1966 the construction of the new Rumtek was complete and the relics brought out from Tsurphu were installed. On Tibetan New Year's day (*losar*) HH the 16th Gyalwa Karmapa officially opened his new seat, called 'The Dharma-chakra Centre, a place of erudition and spiritual accomplishment, the seat of the glorious Karmapa'. This was to be the hub from which Kagyu dharma would spread throughout the world and, step by step, the traditional monastic calendar of special prayers, lama dances, summer rains retreat and so forth was reinstated in that centre-point to ensure the correct spiritual dynamic for the years ahead. Rumtek, the mandala with the Karmapa at its centre, became a very special place, described by many as 'the monastery wreathed in a thousand rays of rainbow light'.

In Sikkim itself the foundations of Kagyu dharma were established. Traditional texts were studied, ordinations performed, tulkus found and enthroned, retreat centres built and texts carved onto wooden blocks for xylographic printing. The kindness of the Bhutanese royal family gave hospitality to the Karmapa's tradition in that country also, with the gift of a palace and a large piece of land upon which to establish a major monastery. Gradually, contacts were made in India and Nepal. At one point, His Holiness had a vision that the construction of many temples and monasteries close to the great stupa at Bodhnath in Nepal (which at the time had little except for the stupa, a temple and a few shops) would greatly help the spread of pure buddhadharma throughout the world. Mainly as a result of the Karmapa's inspiration, many teachers have established monasteries and temples there and it has become an important focus of Tibetan Buddhism.

In 1967 the first Western Tibetan Buddhist centre, named 'Samye Ling' after Samye, the first great monastery of Tibet, was established in Scotland by Trungpa Tulku and Akong Tulku, under the Karmapa's auspices. During the early 70s several other centres emerged in the West and in 1974 the Karmapa set out on his first world tour. I had the pleasure of meeting him at that time and of preparing for his arrival in Scotland and France. The way had already been opened by the visits of the Very Venerable Kalu Rinpoche, whose monks first blew the earth-shaking long horns (*ra-dong*) and oboes (*ja-ling*) of Tibet in Europe. His Holiness's visit set the seal of completion on those first tentative years. Accompanied by tulkus, a full entourage of monks and Freda Bedi, who was now the Buddhist nun Sister Kechog Palmo — 'mummy' to the Tibetans — he performed the Vajra Crown ceremony in our lands for the first time and gave empowerments and dharma advice. In hindsight, that first visit was the milestone which marked the true arrival of the Kagyu tradition in the West.

A great wave of inspiration followed in its wake and His Holiness returned again for a fuller visit in 1977. With many more new centres to visit, this was a very extensive world tour. He visited centres on four continents and met heads of state, heads of religion, elders of many traditions and people from the world of the arts. Sometimes in dharma centres, sometimes in huge public spaces holding crowds of many thousands, he performed the Vajra Crown ceremony, gave empowerments, ordinations, bodhisattva vow and refuge and many blessings to people of all faiths. On looking through hundreds of photographs of these visits, the striking feature is the contagious joy and happiness of His Holiness wherever he went. One of the few things he could say in English was, "Happy?" His joyful, yet nevertheless powerful and authoritative, presence gave many people new to vajrayana the first real chance to meet a perfect guru free to show the blissful liberation of his enlightenment.

During this tour, my wife and I had the honour of accompanying him for six months, I as a visa-seeking cum centre-preparing cum chauffeur factotum for the European stage of his tour, organised by Akong Tulku Rinpoche, and Katia as promoter of a major new monastery and dharma centre to be built on land in France's Dordogne donated by the inventor Bernard Benson. In travelling at the 16th Karmapa's side during that time, through many different countries, I saw him time after time awaken the fundamental goodness and spiritual potential in people. It was like being with the morning sun as it passes over the earth, warming the ground, nourishing life everywhere and opening millions of flowers. Never had any of us met anyone who radiated so much fundamental goodness and joy, who spoke with such natural authority and fearlessness and whose every gesture was the living demonstration of mindfulness, lucidity and compassionate care for everyone. All paled next to the shimmering natural intelligence that he embodied and that seemed to permeate every place in which he stayed.

We had the particular pleasure of helping him buy and look after the birds of which he was so fond. I saw breeders amazed as their normally fearful and hard-to-catch birds went peacefully to the Karmapa. But especially we saw the birds which died stay erect for days in a peaceful glow of meditation on their perches, instead of dropping to the cage floor, as is normal. Some said these birds were reincarnations of former disciples, who through some bad karma had this lesser body but who through their devotion were born into his presence.

Under the Karmapa's overall guidance, the tulkus and rinpoches of the Kagyu tradition nurtured the interest shown by Americans, Europeans and people in South-East Asia in the centres which they had been invited to establish. His Holiness dedicated himself to preparing the essential basis for the proper future growth of this interest, ensuring the education of the younger reincarnated lamas he had recognised, nurturing the growth of the sangha, and sponsoring the collection, translation and printing of the main scriptures and prayers. During his life he ordained many thousands of monks and recognised more than a hundred tulkus. In particular, he sponsored and distributed to many centres a complete reprint of all the Buddha's teachings (*tripitaka*) and the main classical commentaries on them; some 300 volumes of scripture in all.

At one point early in his life, while still in Tibet, His Holiness had written a very telling poem, predicting his leaving Tibet. In it, he uses the analogy of the cuckoo which, in Tibetan folk culture, is known as the king of birds: a welcome bird whose call heralds the warmer weather. It is the bird that grows up in another's nest and the Karmapa, referring to himself as the cuckoo, obviously foresaw his own going to India. During the latter part of the 16th Karmapa's life, people were already impressed by the accuracy of this prediction. Now it is seen to have had a double meaning, as the 17th Karmapa migrates back to the former 'nest' of Tsurphu. Significantly, a cuckoo landed on the tent in which the 17th Karmapa was being born and sang its song.

Great gurus are mirrors reflecting not only their individual disciples' needs but also the general status of things in the world. When their bodies take sick, it can be viewed as being their purification of the sufferings in the world and in their disciples. They also set the example of how to relate to sickness. There is no single interpretation of such things, though, as they are the emanation within our lives of cosmic purity, showing anything that can help us to learn. This is discussed later, in the chapter on Karmapa as buddha nature. However, this type of 'interpretation' could be seen as just wishful thinking, were it not for the miraculous power over the body shown by the Karmapas.

The 16th Karmapa left footprints in rocks on many occasions and in many countries. One day poisonous snakes swarmed from a rock and covered him whilst he was bathing in the Tarzi hot springs, yet he danced joyfully, unharmed. He once tied a heavy sword blade into knots. In his presence, normally antagonistic animals got on well with each other. When photographed with a single plate camera at Rumtek, during an empowerment, he appeared almost transparent *(see photo in colour section)*. Thorough expert checking of the negative and a giant print made from it showed that double exposure or any other normal explanation was impossible. At other times the Karmapa made rain for the Hopi Indians and ended droughts, once by bathing on a chosen spot, whence a spring burst forth. His Holiness also left a footprint in the waters of a Tibetan lake, which can still be seen, summer and winter, as a constant footprint depression in the water. The stories of the physical wonders of the 16th Karmapa, witnessed by Buddhists, are many but perhaps the most striking events were those which took place around his death, for these were witnessed by amazed non-Buddhist physicians in an Illinois hospital.

During the 1970s, the Karmapa started to show signs of cancer. At one point, this became life-threatening and he was operated upon. After a remission, there was a gradual recurrence, complicated by the fact that his symptoms came and went, totally disappeared or manifested as something completely different in a way which confounded regular analysis. He was undoubtedly unwell yet it was as though his body were joking with the machines. His illness was to end in death at the American International Clinic in Zion, near Chicago, Illinois.

Many inexplicable things happened during that time in Illinois. A medical record of them was kept by the Indian army physician Dr Kotwal, who had accompanied His Holiness medically for many years. When the immortal enlightened mind of the 16th Karmapa left its physical shell, his body remained in gentle meditation for three days, during which time the heart centre remained very warm and the skin supple. This was attested to by the doctors despite all the other clinical symptoms of death. Amazed, some of the medical staff visited the holy place of his room to witness the impossible. Only after three such days did the usual manifestations of death appear.

His Holiness's body was flown back to India and cremated in grand ceremony at Rumtek. During the cremation ceremony, each of the four main rinpoches made a mandala offering. When it was the Tai Situpa's turn, he approached the northern gate of the cremation urn to offer the tsampaka flour mandala and saw

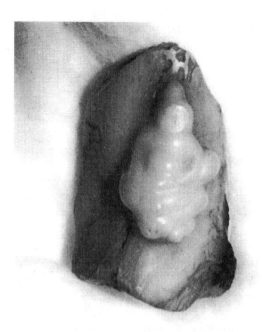

Bone fragment from the body of HH the 16th Karmapa bearing a spontaneously formed Buddha image

something fall from the blazing body onto the base of the inner pyre, near the gate. Unsure what to do for the best, the Tai Situpa quickly sent a monk to ask advice from the Very Venerable Kalu Rinpoche, who was most experienced in such things. Some five minutes later, the monk came back through the crowd with a message from Kalu Rinpoche that it was something very sacred and should be removed and kept as a relic. It was His Holiness's heart, now partially charred. This was enshrined in a golden stupa at Rumtek and has become a Kagyu lineage relic, an object of deep veneration. Some of the bones found among the ashes had self-formed images of the Buddhas on them and there were many small crystal relics, known as *rinsel*. Such occurrences — the heart, the self-formed images and rinsel — were also witnessed at the passing of the very first Karmapa, Dusum Chenpa. Some days after the cremation, Jamgon Kongtrul Rinpoche noticed a baby's footprint in the northern quarter of one of the mandalas arranged for the cremation. Perhaps the 16th Karmapa was already leaving signs of the direction of his next emanation. In fact, in several of his spiritual poem-songs, the 16th Karmapa did leave indications of his next rebirth, as the following reveals:

> *This song is ala thala thala,*
> *Ala is the way it arose.*
> *Thala is the way it is expressed in words.*
> *In a pure land, arrayed as the place called Yulo,*
>
> *On a throne of radiant openness*
> *Is the deity of long life, the mother Lady Tara.*

I pray to her from the centre of my heart.
May there be no obstacles to long life.

If you do not recognise this place,
It is the Retreat Centre of Palpung.
If you do not recognise a person like me,
There is the upper valley of delightful Shukra

And the lower valley of delightful Shukra;
In the place between the two Shukras[1]
Is a child whose father's lineage is 'den and mother's lineage is tsa.
If you call him by name, it is Thubten Gelek.[2]

Not now, but on a distant tomorrow it will be decided.
Both the vulture and I know where to go.
The vulture soars into the expanse of the sky;
Our people do not stay, but go to India.[3]

In the springtime, a cuckoo comes as a guest.
In the fall when the harvest ripens, it knows where to go:
Its only thought is travel to the east of India.[4]
In the lofty land of Tibet, the inhabitants, high and low,

And in particular, you, Tai Situ, the Lord and Protector Maitreya,
Who remains above the crown of our head,
May your activities like the sun and moon set in space
Be continuous, stable, and without hindrance.

I pray that we meet again and again.[5]
The three roots, yidams, and dakinis,
Protect him from negative conditions and obstacles.
Keep the precise meaning recorded here in the depth of your heart.

In the 16th rabjung's [sixty-year cycle's] year of the iron dragon, the 16th incarnation of the Karmapas, Rangjung Rikpe Dorje, composed this song when he was 17 years old at Palpung Chökhor Ling. May it be auspicious.

[1]   This indicates the birthplace of the 17th Karmapa, situated between the two Shukra valleys with a river flowing across one end.

[2]   Thubten Gelek is a childhood name of the 17th Karmapa.

[3]   Here the Karmapa is clearly predicting the future flight of the Tibetans to India.

[4]   Following its pattern of migration, the cuckoo comes in the spring and leaves in the fall; in this same natural way, the Karmapa knows when it is time to leave Tibet for the eastern part of India, where he will take up residence in Rumtek, Sikkim.

[5]   The Karmapa is alluding to the fact that Tai Situ Rinpoche will meet him again as the

17th reincarnation of the Karmapa, Urgyen Trinley Dorje. It is Tai Situ Rinpoche who discovered the 17th Karmapa and takes responsibility for him; thus they meet again and again.

One duty of great spiritual teachers is to discourage disciples from taking their presence for granted. Lord Buddha's passing into nirvana was a formidable teaching given to remind his followers of their own responsibility, to themselves and others, to practise and not always to be carried on the wave of another's spirituality. Lord Buddha's parting words were: "All composite things are impermanent; strive with earnestness." In the passing away and reincarnation of the Karmapa, it is very important for each disciple to learn about impermanence and to pray sincerely and wholeheartedly for the master to reincarnate. Those deep prayers help shake them from the mental lethargy which is a meditator's enemy; the expectation of having everything 'handed to one on a plate', the feeling that someone else will do the necessary. It is important for each person to participate in the calling out for that pure mind to grace the world again. Death is, and will always be, a Buddhist's greatest teacher and it was a painful lesson for many people, including Westerners, when the 16th Karmapa died, or indeed when any other of their beloved teachers dies. The years of uncertainty, longing, praying, reflection before the reincarnation is found bring much maturity to the mind, helping one to appreciate more fully each moment to be spent with fine gurus in the future. Meeting remarkable teachers is a result of excellent past karma, and it is vital to keep generating the karma in the present in order to make such meetings happen again and again in the future. In this process, motivation and heartfelt prayer play a central role.

Marpa the Translator brought the Kagyu dharma to Tibet. His Holiness the 16th Karmapa brought it to the world, turning the wheel of dharma on all its levels and immaculately establishing the right conduct, meditation and wisdom which are the three mainstays of the Buddha's teachings.

Chapter Four

The Meaning of Lineage

". . . The country to the north of this continent
means that Buddha Sakyamuni's teaching will spread through Tibet.
The snow mountain rising above it represents the aged father,
Marpa the Translator and the teachings of all the Kagyu.
The snowy summit touching the heavens is its unrivalled vision of truth.
Sun and moon circling around the mountain peak
are meditation endowed with lucidity, wisdom and compassion.
The lightbeams filling the sky are loving kindness dispelling the darkness
of ignorance . . ."

Extract from Patriarch Marpa's interpretation
of his disciple Milarepa's prophetic dream

There are many enthralling stories to be found in the biographies of the Karmapas. Naturally enough, these fire the imagination and prick our curiosity by opening up the possibility of there being someone who can work wonders — not just in the legends of a distant past but right up to the present day. Fascinating though they may be, it is beyond these anecdotes that the main purpose — and the real impact — of the Karmapas is to be found, in the purity and strength of the teachings they have consistently brought to millions of people over the past nine hundred years, first in Eastern Asia and now throughout the world. At the heart of that far-reaching influence lies the power of lineage.

A lineage is an unbroken transmission of living wisdom. It is living because mastery of the lineage's practices and techniques, which give rise to that wisdom, is perfectly maintained generation after generation. This mastery is handed down through the ages via a succession of highly-accomplished persons, each able to ensure that the integrity of what he or she has received will be carefully passed on to the most gifted disciples, who in turn will do the same. The Karmapas, who are the central force and inspiration of the Karma Kagyu lineage, have been pivotal in maintaining, right up to the present day, the purity of many special teachings originating directly from the Buddha. The majority of these teachings were gathered together more than a thousand years ago in India by Tilopa, Maitripa and other great Buddhist masters of the 11th century.

The Tibetan saint and translator Marpa made three long journeys to India to secure these teachings, knowing they were the heart-essence of Buddhism. His successor, Milarepa, Tibet's most renowned yogin, transmitted them to Gampopa and he in turn to the first Karmapa. The fascinating and inspiring life stories of each of these early Indian and Tibetan patriarchs will be mentioned briefly in a

The Golden Rosary of the Kagyu
The Line of Transmission of the Illustrious Kagyu Teachings through the Karmapas

Name	Karmapa	Situ	Shamar	Gyaltsab	Sanje Nyenpa	Kongtrul
Buddha Vajradhara						
Tilopa						
Naropa						
Marpa		Situ				
Milarepa						
Gampopa						
Dusum Khyenpa	K1					
Drogon Rechen		Situ				
Pomdrakpa						
Karma Pakshi	K2					
Orgyenpa						
Rangjung Dorje	K3					
Yungtonpa						
Rolpi Dorje	K4					
Kacho Wangpo			Shamar 2			
Deshin Shekpa	K5					
Ratnabhadra		Situ				
Tongwa Donden	K6					
Jampal Zangpo						
Paljor Dondrup				Gyaltsab 1		
Chodrak Gyamtso	K7					
Tashi Paljor					Sanje Nyenpa	
Mikyo Dorje	K8					
Konchok Yenlag			Shamar 5			
Wangchuk Dorje	K9					
Choji Wangchuk			Shamar 6			
Choying Dorje	K10					
Yeshe Nyingpo			Shamar 7			
Yeshe Dorje	K11					
Choji Dondrup			Shamar 8			
Changchub Dorje	K12					
Choji Jungnay		Situ 8				
Dundul Dorje	K13					
Mipam Chodrup Gyamtso			Shamar 10			
Pema Nyinche		Situ 9				
Tekcho Dorje	K14					
Yonten Gyamtso						Kongtrul 1
Khachap Dorje	K15					
Pema Wangcho		Situ 11				
Jamgon Chentse Ozer						Kongtrul 2
Rangjung Rikpi Dorje	K16					

Urgyen Trinley Dorje, the 17th Gyalwa Karmapa, is currently in the initial stages of his traditional education, in preparation for eventually receiving the lineage transmissions.

later chapter. They constitute the origin of the Karma Kagyu lineage.

Other lineages, involving meditation, monasticism, yoga, training in compassion and so forth, became integrated into this central lineage and the whole has since been kept vibrantly alive in Tibet by an unbroken succession of spiritual masters, constituted by the seventeen Karmapas and their gurus and known as the Golden Rosary of the Kagyu. The teachings themselves are like the unbroken thread of this rosary. The distinguishing quality of the Karma Kagyu lineage is to have been the first in which the same great spiritual teacher returned again and again — as a reincarnate lama — to nurture his lineage. Although one encounters occasional accounts of Buddhist masters in India being identified as reincarnations of former masters, there was not this custom of systematic return in order to maintain a very special area of teaching. The second Karmapa, Karma Pakshi, was in fact the first to do this; he was the first tulku of Tibet. The value of his action inspired the leaders of other traditions to do likewise and gradually the tulku tradition came into being.

To explore the importance of his lineage, one needs first to understand something of the Buddhism of Tibet. We will approach it through the traditional explanations of Tibetan lamas, such as those given by lamas of the Karma Kagyu lineage. This is, in fact, the only valid — and the only integral — inroad into Tibetan Buddhism we have just now, as our present-day anthropological, archaeological and historical knowledge of Tibet is still poor and riddled with errors.

Although Tibet embodies a very unique form of Buddhism it is, almost in totality, not Tibetan Buddhism but the Buddhism of 8th-12th century India, transplanted into Tibet in a very extensive and vigorous way throughout those four centuries, both by Indian teachers visiting Tibet and by Tibetans going to India to seek teachings. This turned out to be extremely fortunate, as later, in the twelfth century, India completely lost Buddhism after some fifteen hundred years of being its guardian. During that time, the spread of Buddhism had led to various Buddhist traditions emerging as far afield as Greece to the West and Japan to the East. These grew up, each in their own way, according to specific teachings collected by pilgrims from those lands who had visited the sub-continent. Not everything they took home proved acceptable and, inevitably, the cultural susceptibilities of their own people had a great influence on what managed to take root.

As centuries passed, the Buddhism of Sri Lanka, China, Japan and other countries took shape. But nowhere was such a range of Buddhist teachings and traditions to be found as in Tibet. It is almost as though the snowy land at the roof of the world became the deep-freeze that preserved the vast array of Buddhism which was flourishing in India at the time of Tibet's conversion, a thousand years ago. Despite the physical barrier of the Himalayas, Tibet's relative proximity to the great centres of Buddhist learning in Kashmir, Bengal and Central India and the sheer number of famous teachers who plied back and forth enabled a complete transplantation of India's Buddhism to take place. It is even tempting to think that many of the great Indian and Tibetan masters involved in establishing Buddhism in Tibet somehow knew it was their duty to make sure that everything was secured for the future. The single-mindedness which is typical of Tibetans, their tremendous respect for their religion and the relative stability of their culture, little troubled by the great movements agitating the outer world, no doubt all contributed to the way in which Buddhism then remained unchanged in the land of snows.

Whatever it was that really happened in those important moments of Buddhist history, it is certainly the case that in Tibetan Buddhism we find gathered together all the main practices and philosophical traditions which exist severally in Sri Lanka, Burma, Thailand, Korea, China, Japan, Mongolia and other Buddhist countries. Furthermore we find that aspect of Indian Buddhism known as the indestructible way or vajrayana which does not seem to be widely extant anywhere other than in Tibet.

To those who penetrate its meaning, the completeness of Tibetan Buddhism is something very joyous. It is like the relief of becoming the patient of a doctor who has a complete pharmacopoeia at his disposal, whereas hitherto in one's travels one only found this or that medicine available and had to make do. Indeed, the medical analogy is pertinent, the task of a lama being a very holistic one; rather than having just one partisan line of religious advice to give, the lama draws on a very broad bank of remedies which help the whole person in whichever way is best suited to the circumstances.

That Tibetan Buddhism is the most complete Buddhism to be found is a point which needs to be made, as many people might otherwise imagine it to be a rather specialised and limited backwater. In particular, from looking at its iconography in illustrated books and elsewhere, those unaware of its real Indian origin have assumed that it is a weird hybrid of Indian Buddhism, ancient Tibetan shamanism and Hindu tantra. This is as naïve as seeing the plaids they weave in Bhutan and assuming that therefore they must have been invaded by the Scots at some time in the past! Serious consideration of the tenets of Tibetan Buddhist philosophy brings one to realise the sheer philosophical impossibility of any such hybrid faith. Hinduism is deeply theistic. Shamanism is, by its very nature, rooted in the reality of natural forces. Yet Buddhism has non-theism and irreality (voidness) of things at the very heart of its compassionate philosophy.

What does constantly occur in teaching Buddhism is a need to express ideas through an imagery which makes real sense to people. If the Buddha had to teach a potter, he might well have used the potter's wheel and clay as examples to bring a point home vividly. This does not mean he invented a new pottero-Buddhist religion. Indian tantric Buddhism seems to have expressed traditional Buddhist values through ritualistic mechanisms and gestures familiar to the Indian people from their existing religions, yet all the time retaining its own ethics and philosophy.

◆ ◆ ◆

Tibetan Buddhism can be viewed as having three main levels of teaching, compared very wittily by the late Kalu Rinpoche to a saucer, a teacup and the tea. The basis — the saucer — for all traditions of Buddhism throughout the world is summed up by the famous couplet:

> *"To refrain from all harm, to do whatever is good*
> *and to tame one's mind — this is the teaching of the Buddhas."*

To *refrain from all harm* is the famous Buddhist path of non-aggression. It means finding the way of no longer causing pain, either to others or oneself. This requires some understanding of the longer-term consequences of action (karma) and is achieved practically by cultivating a natural dignity of conduct. It mainly involves making, and subsequently keeping, strong personal commitments to living a life that is noble in action and pure in intent. The purpose of lay and monastic vows is to help strengthen one's resolve in this.

In times such as ours, in which the tendency is to self-gratification and exploitation of the world's resources, it is already something very positive to be able to avoid doing harm. The Buddha himself stressed that in the sixth 500-year period after his passing, i.e. our present age, it would be a powerful virtue in itself to maintain a pure conduct. The next step on from that is to *do whatever is good*. This involves learning to use body and speech in a positive way at all times, turning them into a constant source of well-being. Finally, *one's mind can be tamed* gradually by training in meditation and by developing a very frank insight into the human condition. In particular, the calming of one's mind brings one to understand that all personality projections are no more than conditioned illusions to which one has become very accustomed and attached. Beyond the ego's tiresome attempts to exist, there is a profound and constant peace, replete with more qualities than the ego could ever dream of. This is called wisdom of non-ego or voidness of ego.

To return to our analogy: the above foundation was like the saucer. Relying on and supported by it is — the teacup, a noble and precious container — a life totally dedicated to the welfare of others and to discovering the ultimate truth of existence. This is the greater way or mahayana, in which ultimate wisdom, also known as voidness wisdom, encompasses not only the ego but everything and anything that the mind can experience. Those who follow this way are called bodhisattva. Besides developing wisdom, they are dedicated to bringing five areas of their lives to perfection:

— generosity,
— pure conduct in whatever they do,
— forbearance,
— enthusiastic dedication and
— mastery of meditation.

These five are known as paramita, which translates loosely as 'transcendent perfection', and collectively are called skilful means. The consummate fusion of skilful means with wisdom (which is the sixth paramita, famous as the prajñaparamita) is the aim of mahayana Buddhism, which was practised mainly in Tibet, Mongolia, China, Korea and Japan.

Finally, the precious essence — the warm, nourishing and delicious tea — contained within the greater way is the powerful technique of vajrayana, which enables all life's circumstances to be transformed into a path of profound spirituality. Just as the tea is the very raison d'être for the cup and the saucer, so is the vajrayana the final meaning of all Buddhism. It survived on a large scale and in its original form mainly in Tibet, whence it influenced many Asian countries in centuries gone by. This century it has been found principally in Tibet, Mongolia, Bhutan and neighbouring Himalayan areas.

If the vast wealth of Buddhist teaching preserved and practised in Tibet were to be compared to a kingdom, the Karmapa would be its timeless king, returning again and again to ensure its prosperity. He is the one who maintains the clarity, the power and the purity of these three levels of Buddhism by revivifying their truths from generation to generation. This is signified by his name. Karma means 'action' or 'activity' in Sanskrit and this is made into a substantive in Tibetan by adding the syllable pa. He is thus named because, like an ambassador, he is the one empowered in our world to accomplish the activity of all the Buddhas, and in particular of Buddha Sakyamuni. Although the latter passed away over two-and-a-half thousand years ago, his guiding influence continues to be active on Earth for some five thousand years after his passing, and the Karmapa is one of the key beings entrusted with the task of keeping things on course as age leads to age, through his enlightened activity. His name could have been fully translated into Tibetan as Trinleypa (*phrin.las.pa*) (the same Trinley as in the present Karmapa's name) but has been kept partly in Sanskrit to remind us that his lives, as the 'one of karma' — the Karmapa, were predicted by the Buddha Sakyamuni in teachings such as the samadhirajasutra (see Chapter 8), which were first written down in a form of Sanskrit.

Whoever has carefully observed relations between spiritual teachers and their students will appreciate the value of this revitalising presence. Once someone has received inspiring guidance, the unfortunate tendency is gradually, almost imperceptibly, to forget it; or worse, to reinterpret it into something more personally convenient. Like a picked flower, the original inspiration and clarity can fade; like a vivid day in the country, it becomes merely a memory; like Chinese whispers, the message gradually changes. Teachers have a sacred duty to convey certain truths and much of their actual teaching task involves refreshing their disciples' awareness of those truths in a process of continual reawakening. This is necessary not only for individuals but also, as social and monastic attitudes change from generation to generation, for whole societies through those with great responsibilities, such as the Karmapa.

◆ ◆ ◆

Here we return to the original point. The actual way in which the integrity and purity of all three levels of Buddhist teachings has been maintained is through lineage, in the broadest sense of the term, where it is applicable to all three levels. One of the oldest lineages is the transmission of the ability to ordain people or give them lay precepts. This was handed down from the Buddha to his followers and then from them to their own disciples and so on, right up to the present day. Important in this process is not just the perpetuation of a formal power to ordain but the fact that the person giving the vows actually keeps them and understands them himself or herself. Transmission involves the outer form and the inner spirit both being kept alive; practising what is preached.

Living lineage is a fragile thing. Once the chain of succession is broken, it can only be restored by reconnecting with another transmission from the same source and which is still intact — and then integrating that lineage into one's own. An interesting example of this happened with the lineage for full nun's (bhikkhuni) vows which did not persist in Tibet. Tibetan nuns were either siksamana or sramanerika. After leaving Tibet and finding the existence of bhikkhuni lineage in Asia, the 16th Gyalwa Karmapa was keen that nun's full ordination be eventually reintegrated into his tradition.

Other than this one exception, the remaining levels of monk, nun and lay precepts were widely maintained in Tibet. Some estimate that up to a quarter of its male population, and somewhat less of the female population, lived the monastic life. Many of the remaining population observed lay precepts.

The Buddha taught that the healthy survival of his teachings through the ages depends upon the sangha (community of monks and nuns) remaining strong. For nine centuries the Karmapas have been a major force in Eastern Asia, fostering and spreading the basic teachings of Buddhism, establishing monasteries, nunneries, temples and retreat centres and inspiring literally millions to be less obsessed by the world of materiality and to seek their mind's true peace. Besides this, they have created the material reminders necessary for an eventual realisation of immaterial enlightenment, by building stupas, Buddha images and other representations as well as establishing printing houses in which the classical texts could be carved onto wood blocks and printed. They themselves have composed many texts and prayers elucidating the mainstream of Buddhist teachings. In brief, in terms of lineage, they have perpetuated the existing lineages of the general level of Buddhism and, by embodying the activity-aspect of the Buddhas, established a rich heritage of traditions within the monastic arts of prayer, music, iconography and so forth.

The Karmapas have also maintained the lineages of mahayana, the greater way. There are two main traditions of taking the bodhisattva vow, which is the point of entry into mahayana, and of working towards enlightenment. One goes back to the Indian mahasiddha Nagarjuna and the other to the great Indian saint and scholar Asanga. These traditions are seen as having their origins in the celestial bodhisattvas Manjusri and Maitreya respectively. The former is famous for the profundity of its teachings on voidness; the illusory nature of everything. It is called the deep tradition. The latter is famous for the vastness of its teachings on the way all sorts of people can gradually mature in compassion; it is called the vast tradition. Although these are their names and their reputation, both traditions are, in practice, very complete in their approach to voidness and the graduated path. Each has been carefully maintained as a valuable part of the teaching wealth of the Kagyu tradition

There are literally hundreds of classical scriptures in mahayana Buddhism, many of them written in verse. Some describe, in very human terms, the power, the necessity and the nature of compassion. Others describe the experiential possibilities of the mind as it sheds its illusions and then progresses through ten long-lasting levels in which everything always manifests as purity. Because delusions of ego have to be abandoned even to penetrate the first of these levels, the mind during those stages is remarkably free and in constant contact with the universality of enlightenment. Therefore it can experience thousands of realities simultaneously, each pure, clear and meaningful. The actual experience of those levels is quite inconceivable and the texts can refer to them only very sketchily.

The Karmapas, who are seen as being themselves on the tenth and last level and thus having direct knowledge of those states, are therefore ideal lineage holders of the mahayana aspect of Buddhism within their Kagyu tradition. In practice, they have maintained a living transmission of insight into the real meaning behind the classical explanations found within the vast canon of bodhisattva literature. As they embody the bodhisattva ideal in their own lives, they have kept the torch of its inspiration aglow, not just in their role as religious patriarchs but also as mediators between governments and as peacemakers in general.

Finally, and perhaps most importantly, the Karmapas are the custodians of many vajrayana lineages: those proper to the Karma Kagyu tradition and others too. This very special role of the Karmapa will be discussed at length in Chapter 8, which describes the Buddha's predictions in the samadhirajasutra; in Chapter 9, on the Kagyu tradition; and in Chapter 10, on vajrayana.

Chapter 5

Finding the new Karmapa

Finding reincarnate lamas

When a very respected Tibetan lama dies, his reincarnation, called a *tulku*, can be found in a variety of ways. His disciples might consult an eminent lama of their particular tradition, hoping for him to give some indication of the time and place of rebirth, either through natural clairvoyance or clairvoyance brought about by deep meditation. It might also happen that a gifted child, or talk of him, comes to the attention of someone competent, who realises that he is the reincarnation of such and such a lama. Signs can occur in lamas' dreams, or through special divination ceremonies. In some traditions the child, once found, is subjected to a series of clever tests, carried out to confirm the identification. A typical test might be to place an object belonging to the previous incarnation among a dozen or so similar objects and then to ask the child to choose one.

Unlike all other tulkus, a Karmapa is found through signs that he himself provides, most often in written form, such as a letter. Thus the 17th Karmapa was discovered according to guidance he himself had written down in Calcutta in January 1981, in a letter he concealed in an amulet he made, which he gave to the 12th Tai Situpa, saying that it would protect him and would one day prove very beneficial.

The written previsions of the Karmapa may of course tally with the clear vision of a great lama. Furthermore, it has even been known for past Karmapas to set

The search party — Akong Rinpoche (left) and Sherab Tarchin (right) with the 17th Karmapa's father

out all on their own to meet their gurus and thus manifest their presence. Some Karmapas have been recorded as declaring "I am the Karmapa" at birth or soon afterwards, sometimes sitting up in meditation. This is highly reminiscent of Buddha Sakyamuni himself, when immediately after birth he took seven steps in each of the cardinal directions, intermediate directions, and nadir and zenith, with lotuses springing up beneath his feet, and declared in a lion-like roar, "I am the Lord of the World." In fact, it also says in the *Lalitavistara* that in each direction he made a pun on the name saying, for instance, "This is the supreme direction," when he took his steps to the north, as the words for 'north' and 'supreme' sound the same. Having cast his divine gaze through the length and breadth of the cosmos in each of the ten directions, and seeing no one his equal, he declared his supremacy. This fearless confidence in declaring his uniqueness, so doing without any defilement of pride, is one of the 32 qualities of a Buddha.

This sort of thing is difficult for the materialist to understand. How can the untrained vocal cords of a newly-born baby enunciate such words? How can lotuses spring up in seconds? Like the answers to so many similar doubts, the answer to these questions lies in the very nature of perception, as modern science is beginning to understand. Science is no longer the yardstick for measuring a concrete common universe, but the common language through which one person can communicate his or her personal perception of the universe to another. Each person's moment-to-moment experience is quite unique and our parallel worlds of experience only overlap within the abstractions of language.

Normal perception depends upon the quality of the perceiver and the nature of the perceived. Both sides of the perceptive process have their limits. What I see of a flower is determined both by what it has to show and by the sharpness of my eyesight. But when the perceived is itself the unlimited ultimate perfection of mind, so many subjective impressions of it are possible. Thus, hundreds of people can perceive spontaneous lotuses or see a rain of flowers. From that point of view, there are no miracles in Buddhism, only usual or un-usual phenomena, but all of them due to their specific causes; all of them the play of interdependence at work in the human psyche.

For reasons best known to the clear mind of the Karmapas themselves, they give a prediction letter to a trusted disciple, with confidential instructions as to when to act, or else they conceal it somewhere to be found at an appropriate time. The discovery of the 16th Gyalwa Karmapa was an interesting case in point. The 15th Karmapa had entrusted an amulet to Jampel Tsultim, his closest attendant, telling him to open it at a time when there would be some events occurring involving Palpung monastery. After Kachab Dorje's death, Jampel Tsultim returned to a nomadic area. As time went by, the 11th Tai Situpa recognised the new Karmapa in the A-toop family and sent a representative, Lama Lodro, to Tsurphu. The latter, accompanied by the Tsurphu General Secretary, Dechang, sought advice and a decision on the reincarnation from HH the Dalai Lama in Lhasa. Some four years passed before the Dalai Lama granted confirmation. Jampel Tsultim heard about the petitioning from Palpung and returned to offer the amulet to the Tsurphu authorities, who relayed it to Palpung. The Tai Situpa opened it only to find it all written in unusual symbolic letters on a long piece of Tibetan paper. By this time HH the Karmapa was already enthroned and at Palpung. One of the main tulkus at Palpung was Beru Khyentse Rinpoche. His cook, who was unwell, had gone to circumambulate De-ge Printing Place (considered a very holy spot). He saw a page of text being blown around on the ground and picked it up out of respect, as is Buddhist custom. Looking at it, he discovered it to be part of a text containing the cyphers needed for decoding the particular symbolic script contained in the 15th Karmapa's letter and he gave it to his guru. When Beru Khyentse Rinpoche and the Tai Situpa worked out the meaning of the testamentary letter, they found that it accorded with the details of the new Karmapa.

Finding the 17th Karmapa

During the 1980s, the four main tulkus and other persons close to the late 16th Karmapa sought his prediction letter for years, trying to remember all His Holiness's words and to think of clues that might lead them to the sacred document. It was only in late 1990/early 1991 that the Tai Situpa, while in retreat, recalled the small golden pouch that the Karmapa had given him in Calcutta in 1981 as a protection. One normally never opens such a protection, which is stitched closed, but somehow the Situpa was inspired to investigate. The letter was indeed inside, with instructions for it not to be opened before the Iron Horse year (1990-91). The Tai Situpa's inspiration had been timely and in accord with the wishes of the 'Knower of the Three Times'. Even had the letter been found many years previously, everyone would have had to wait until 1990 for it to be opened.

The Tai Situpa informed the other three main tulkus of his find and they met in Rumtek on March 29, 1992 to read and interpret its message. It gave clear indications of the birthplace and parents of the new Karmapa, saying:

E MA HO Auto-cognisant, universal bliss, dharmadhatu free from centre or extremity. In the east of the snows to the north of here, in thunder-god[1] land which blazes, in a beautiful nomad's place called 'easily-milked'[2], the skilful means is dondrup and the wisdom is lolaga. In the year of the one who labours the earth[3], the wondrous one, the far-sounding white one. The one known as the Karmapa, greatly renowned will be nurtured by the illustrious Donyö Drup[4]. In a way which pervades every quarter, without bias, closeness or remoteness, the protector of beings, through the blazing of the sun benefiting others, the Victor's teachings.

1   god is *lha* in Tibetan and thunder is *thog*. Together they make Lhathog, the area of the Karmapa's birth.

2   The Easily-Milked One is a traditional epithet for a cow. Cow is *ba* in Tibetan and the nomadic settlement where the Karmapa was born is called Ba-kor.

3   The one who labours the earth is the ox. The ox year was 1985.

4   The Tai Situpa's dharma name, given to him by the previous Gyalwa Karmapa, was Pema Donyö, the first indicating him as an emanation of Guru Rinpoche and the second relating him to Amogasiddhi (Tib: *don.yod.grub*).

There is however a deeper set of meanings to be read into these words, revealed by the Goshir Gyaltsabpa in his commentary *The Sun of Mind* .

Prediction letter written by the 16th Karmapa, found in the Tai Situpa's amulet

'The Sun of Mind'

*A word-by-word commentary on the prediction letter of the Supreme Victor,
the 16th Karmapa*

The syllables *E MA HO* — how wondrous! — *commence it with auspiciousness*. *Auto-cognisant* innate primordial wisdom, through its spontaneous, uninterrupted and limitless activity to effortlessly teach sentient beings has *universal* great *bliss* as its very nature, this being the facet of skilful means.

Dharmadhatu, which is neither fused with, nor separate from, that is *free from* any conceptualisation of *centre* or *extremity*. Therefore, although it does not intentionally contemplate either taking birth in worlds where actions are difficult, or the quantities of beings to be helped, or the duration of the ages it might take, nevertheless that which is unborn appears to the various beings being helped as taking birth and so forth. It is not substantially real, as something other in its own right. This is the facet of profound wisdom.

The two phrases depicting these two facets show that which is utterly pure, in the certainty of ultimate truth, manifesting within the expedient truth as two.

Then, through kingly bodhicitta which is fully endowed with clear cognition, it speaks of his future manifestation which will create a mighty wave of benefit for conscious beings.

From this dharmachakra seat of meditation achievement and erudition, *in the east of the snows to the north*, externally there is a land sustained by the mighty miraculous transformation of the *thunder*-accompanied wrathful deities and the good and benevolent *deities*. Internally and secretly, it is in *a land which* possesses the deities' mandala, the foundation in which *blaze* the nine aspects of the mandala which is the basis of that which exists of itself and by itself since time immemorial.

In that land, in a *beautiful nomad place denoted* by the name of the *one milked at will*, the *skilful means*, i.e. father, will be named *dondrup* and the wisdom, i.e. mother, *lolaga*. From the perfection of the tenth bodhisattva level in the buddha-palace of her womb, and from the motherly space of the dharmasambhava, in the *year of the one who works the earth* will emerge the *wondrous* nirmanakaya accompanied by the sign which is the sound of the *far-sounding white one*, the conch, because he will outshine all those who pronounce falsely. He will become *the one known as the Karmapa, greatly renowned* in an ocean of buddhafields. Although within him the primordial wisdoms of the four empowerments are already perfected, it will be necessary for him to be empowered into the enlightened means of the vajra-master and in this he will *be nurtured* by the Tai Situ, who bears the name of the *illustrious Dönyö Drup* pa (Amogasiddhi). This is in accordance with the predictions made by Chojur Lingpa through his clear visions.

The special quality of his enlightened activity towards those karmically ready will be to turn the wheel of dharma *in a way which pervades every quarter* and in a way which is *without bias*. Since he is without *closeness or remoteness* in sentiment towards those less ready, he will manage to sow the seeds of liberation in them by using many sorts of skills. Thus he will be the *protector of* all *beings* without exception.

In brief, *through the blazing of the sun* which is the vast *benefiting of others, the Victorious One's teachings* dispel the darkness of ignorance, and the brilliance of the kayas and wisdom flourishes.

The above was composed in the town of Balpo Yambu by Gyaltsab Minjur Gocha on the 14th day of the 6th month according to the interpretation that arose in his mind.

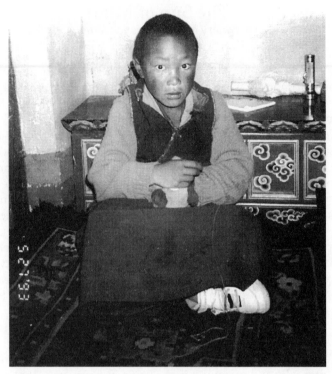

Apo Gaga during the very first days of his discovery by the search party

In the light of these clear indications, it was agreed that Jamgön Kongtrul Rinpoche would go to Tibet on behalf of all of them to confirm the indications of the letter. Not long after setting out on April 26th, in a newly-serviced BMW lent to him for the journey, Jamgön Kongtrul Rinpoche and some of his attendants were killed outright in a disastrous early morning crash. This shattering event caused terrible sadness throughout the Kagyu world. Arrangements were made to perform the major rites befitting the passing of a great lama of his status.

Amongst all the lamas who came to pay homage to Kongtrul Rinpoche's remains, Akong Tulku Rinpoche arrived in Rumtek on May 1st to participate in the ceremonies for one week on behalf of his organisations. This proved highly opportune. Akong Rinpoche's life's work had been devoted to the Karmapa and the 16th Karmapa had entrusted him with many tasks, including the organisation of his major European tour in 1977. He had also been one of the few lamas to receive the special protector transmissions from His Holiness (see previous chapter). Through his frequent visits to Tibet for his charitable projects which established education, health-care and medical schools in rural areas, he was more aware than anyone of prevailing conditions there. He made the ideal emissary for the delicate mission of seeking out and discovering the Karmapa. The Tai Situpa and the Goshir Gyaltsabpa suggested that he should go, on the Situpa's behalf, and it was agreed that Sherab Tarchin should accompany him, representing the

His Holiness and Amdo Palden, Abbot of Kalek monastery

Goshir Gyaltsabpa, of whose organisation he is the treasurer. Akong Rinpoche, surprised and somewhat unprepared for this historic task, willingly agreed to go.

The first purpose of their visit was to inform the various monasteries of Jamgön Kongtrul Rinpoche's death and to represent the two rinpoches during the 49 days of special prayers in monasteries and sacred places, traditional after the passing of such a holy person. Implicitly understood, though it had at first to be kept secret, was a duty to find the young Karmapa, according to the prediction letter, and to present him with the objects of *tru-sol:* the golden robes, silk scarves and so forth that are given to the young incarnate at the time of recognition. These were prepared by the Tai Situpa and the Goshir Gyaltsabpa and carried by Akong Rinpoche and Sherab Tarchin.

On the way to Tibet, while awaiting visas in Nepal, Akong Rinpoche sent word to Tsurphu monastery, along with a copy of the prediction letter, so that an advance reconnaissance party could investigate and report their findings to him. Thus from Tsurphu, the traditional seat of the Karmapa in central Tibet which, like a phoenix, was gradually arising from the ruins of its former self, a search party consisting of Lama Domo, representing Tsurphu, and others set out to quietly ascertain whether or not there was someone corresponding to the letter's details. They pretended to be carrying letters from relatives in India for a Mr Loga. This was, of course, the mother's name but it made a useful subterfuge for being informed that there was no man Loga but a woman named Loga. Loga and Lola-ga (the name in the prediction letter) mean the same thing; one is simply a con-traction of the other. Asking after her husband's name, they discovered it to be Dondrup, as in the letter, and that they had indeed had a son born in the Wood

Ox year (1985); a very special boy born among many miraculous signs. The search party reported back to Akong Rinpoche and Sherab Tarchin in Chamdo. At the same time, the Tai Situpa and Gyaltsabpa were informed. Every detail of the letter had proven exactly correct, and Akong Rinpoche and Sherab Tarchin felt deeply moved and amazed to realise how, a decade earlier, the 16th Karmapa had foreseen it all so precisely. The young Karmapa was accompanied from his home to Kalek monastery by the advance search party. Akong Rinpoche and Sherab Tarchin presented him there with the golden robes and sacred offerings prepared by the Tai Situpa and the Goshir Gyaltsabpa, thereby completing the formalities of recognition. The Karmapa had been discovered.

On June 7th, 1992 the Tai Situpa and the Goshir Gyaltsabpa went to the bureau of HH the Dalai Lama in Dharamsala to inform him of all the details of the Karmapa incarnation and to ask him to confirm it through the clarity of his profound wisdom. Although he was visiting Brazil at the time, his staff informed him of the news and he confirmed the recognition of Urgyen Trinley Dorje as the new Karmapa, adding that it tallied with a vision he had had personally, some months before, of the Karmapa's birthplace. HH the Dalai Lama had seen, in the crystal lucidity of his mind, green mountains covered with meadows. To the right and left of a valley in the vision were two streams and in the air resounded the name *Karmapa*. He had effectively described the valley in Tibet where Urgyen Trinley

The area of the 17th Karmapa's birth, as seen by the Dalai Lama in a vision

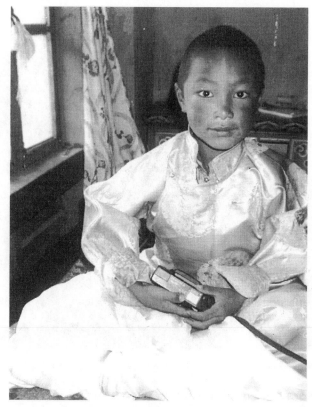

After formal recognition and presentation of the 'golden robes' of a tulku

was born. His Holiness Sakya Trizin, head of the Sakya lineage, and HH Mindroling Trichen, head of the Nyingma lineage, also both confirmed the recognition of the new Karmapa and composed long-life prayers for him.

After spending a little while together and making arrangements, Akong Rinpoche, Sherab Tarchin and a new party from Tsurphu monastery accompanied the Karmapa to Tsurphu, where he would be enthroned. In the meantime, Tsurphu monastery had received permission from the local authorities for their search and discovery and they were allowed to prepare to enthrone the new Karmapa in grand ceremony.

A small faction of people, consisting of the 11th Shamarpa, the 16th Karmapa's nephew — the former monk Topga-la, and their followers had been putting up some resistance to the 16th Karmapa's testamentary letter and the recognition of Dondrup and Loga's son as the new Karmapa. This continued, despite the fact that the issue was technically resolved by the Shamarpa having given his own written agreement to the recognition after being strongly advised so to do by his guru, Urgyen Rinpoche. On the morning of June 29th, the Tai Situpa and the Goshir Gyaltsabpa were received in personal audience by HH the Dalai Lama at Dharamsala. That afternoon, he received the Shamarpa. The following day, HH the Dalai Lama issued his sacred letter of recognition and approval of Dondrup

HH the Dalai Lama issuing his formal recognition letter — the Buktam Rinpoche

and Loga's son, there resolving the issue clearly once and for all. The sealed recognition of the authenticity issued by a Dalai Lama is called a *Buktam Rinpoche* (*sbug.tham.rin.po.che*) in Tibetan. It said:

> The son born to Karma Dondrup and Loga in the Wood Ox year accords with the testament (of the late Karmapa) and is hereby recognised as the reincarnation of the Sixteenth Karmapa. With prayers for his well-being and the success of his sacred activity.
>
> *Third day of fourth month of the Water Monkey year,*
> *June 30th, 1992*

HH the Dalai Lama also gave a blessing scarf, cord and a present of his personal rosary for the Karmapa and made a taped message for followers of the Kagyu tradition, which was broadcast on All India Radio. The following is a translation of his talk:

Brief Advice to Kagyu Followers from His Holiness the Dalai Lama

Translated from His Message
To Tai Situ Rinpoche and Goshir Gyaltsap Rinpoche
Taped on June 30th 1992, 10:45am in Dharamsala

It is mainly Situ Rinpoche, along with Tsurphu Gyaltsap Rinpoche and those closely connected, who are responsible for finding the reincarnation of Gyalwa Karmapa Rinpoche and I am very happy about this. The Gyalwa Karmapa is a supreme master of Buddhist teachings in general, a magnificent lama of Tibet, and in particular of the Kagyu tradition's Karma Kamtsang lineage. To have found his reincarnation therefore is a great benefit for Buddhism in general and for the Kagyu lineage in particular, and so I am very happy.

In Tibetan, there is a proverb that says where there is great Dharma, there is immense Mara, and so there has been a little disharmony and some difficult situations, but these do not have great importance. What is important is the focus on what has real and profound significance, Until now you have worked, keeping in mind what is most important and essential, and you should continue to focus on what is vital, what is crucial.

In the world today, many people have an active interest in Buddhist teachings in general, and especially in Eastern philosophy, and particularly in the teachings of Tibetan Buddhism, which bring together the sutra and tantra traditions. In the future, there will be more people who have this interest. The activities of the previous 16th Gyalwa Karmapa were most successful; he planted the roots of Dharma and the Buddha's teachings generally flourished. At such a time, we Buddhists, who follow the same teacher, Shakyamuni Buddha, and count ourselves his disciples, should continuously maintain pure vision and serve the teachings well, so that numberless sentient beings may always enjoy the source of happiness. We usually pray that the teachings will help all sentient beings; if this is not immediately possible, then at least we can help those on this earth, and especially human beings. This is very important, and so everyone should do whatever possible not to harm others and to travel the noble path of peace.

I pray that this precious reincarnation will have a long life and that his activity, as that of the previous incarnation of the Gyalwa Karmapa, will flourish for the benefit of the teachings and sentient beings. Whatever his wishes are, may they be spontaneously accomplished. I wish you all Tashi Delek.

Chapter Six

HH the 17th Gyalwa Karmapa
Urgyen Trinley Dorje

The parents of the present Karmapa, Dondrup and Loga, are nomads. Their life tending the family herd of some eighty yaks takes them from grazing area to grazing area, according to the humours of the four seasons. They are respected members of a group of some seventy nomadic families; more than four hundred persons, deeply-tanned with apple-red cheeks, whose encampments are a travelling village of felt tents made from long yak hair.

As is customary, Dondrup and Loga dedicated their first son to their local Nyingmapa monastery — Kampagar, one of Khamtrul Rinpoche's monasteries — to be a future monk. They subsequently had five children, all daughters. Longing for another son, they sought help from Karma Norzang, the renowned yogi of Kampagar, reputed to be like a second Milarepa. He advised them to do a hundred thousand refuge prayers, feed beggars, feed the fish in the rivers and go on pilgrimage to Lhasa. These things they did as best they could but, as destiny would have it, any benefit they produced was not to take effect immediately and their next child was yet another daughter.

Loga and Dondrup, the parents of the 17th Karmapa

By the time they were contemplating another attempt at having a son, Karma Norzang had died and so they consulted Amdo Palden, the yogi abbot of Kalek, a Karma Kagyu monastery which formerly belonged to the King of Lhatok. At first Amdo Palden was not sure he could help but, upon further reflection, said that it might be possible for them to have a son but that they must promise to place him, should they have one, in his charge. They agreed to this. His way of helping was to confer empowerment upon them.

During her next pregnancy Loga dreamt of three white cranes offering her a bowl of yoghurt. A brilliant golden letter sat atop the bowl and signified her forth-coming son. The cranes told her that they were sent by Guru Rinpoche and that the golden letter was the recognition letter for her son but that she should keep this information secret until the right time came. At another time she dreamt of eight auspicious symbols wreathed in rainbow light emanating from her heart. The night before the birth, in late June 1985, the father saw rainbows over the tent and was surprised, for the sun had already disappeared behind the mountains. The baby was born the next day without pain or difficulty, just before the first golden rays of sunlight burst into the tent. At the same time, a cuckoo landed on the yak-hair tent and sang. Two days later, the celestial sound of a conch shell, prophesied by the 16th Karmapa in his letter, was heard by all the members of the nomadic community. Those outside their tents thought it came from the inside, and vice versa. Some thought a whole monastic orchestra must be accompany-ing a high lama but none could be seen. It continued through the afternoon for some two hours. Unknown flowers blossomed in the area and, some while later, three suns were seen in the heavens, a rainbow arching over the middle one. This last phenomenon was widely witnessed throughout eastern Tibet.

When Dondrup and Loga went to Amdo Palden to request a Buddhist name for their son, as is the Tibetan custom, he told them that this very special child should not be named by any ordinary abbot. He said that only a very great being, such as the Tai Situpa, could name him and that they should wait until such time as this proved possible. For need of some provisional name, they used one that their daughter said she was given for him by a magpie at a riverside, just after the birth: 'Apo Gaga', meaning 'happy, happy brother'.

As a very young child, Apo Gaga was obviously a very special being, gifted with clairvoyance and authority. He was able, for instance, to tell people where to find lost sheep or cattle. As one might expect, his parents' local monastery of Kampagar wanted to care for him and to give him the special training which would make him a lama to help many beings. But at that point Amdo Palden reminded the parents of their promise and took Apo Gaga under his own care at Kalek monastery. Being more distant from their encampments, this was less con-venient but they nevertheless honoured their commitment and placed Apo Gaga in his care. When asked about the boy, a local oracle, gifted in a form of divina-tion known as 'mirror seeing', saw the form of a white conch with a clockwise

The family of HH the 17th Karmapa

spiral. He predicted that Apo Gaga would greatly benefit sentient beings but that his destiny would not become clear until he was eight years old. Tibetans count a person's age as 'first year' — one — at birth and then add one year as each Tibetan New Year passes. This can result in as much as a year's discrepancy compared with the Western way of counting.

The young Apo Gaga spent about four years receiving a special education at Kalek, where he was given the attention due to an unrecognised reincarnate lama. He had a small throne to one side of the shrine hall and an attendant to help him, and he was not allowed to get up to the same pranks and games as the other young novices, who showed him a great deal of respect. During this phase, he spent moments back with his family in their nomadic round. In those periods, his parents report, he would often build toy monasteries from earth and stone, or else make a small throne and sit on it to recite prayers. They say he would ride off into the hills on the backs of goats or wild animals, that he would cry whenever animals were hurt or killed and that he always showed compassion. He showed a particular interest in trees, frequently planting them and being upset if he saw trees or plant life being destroyed. It is said that springs often emerged where he had planted small clumps of trees.

In 1992 he insisted, without explaining why, that his parents move to their summer pasture one month earlier than they had intended. In the Tibetan calendar, summer is a 72-day period commencing three lunar months after Tibetan New Year. Thus, summer usually starts some time in May. Trusting Apo Gaga's advice, they moved camp early and it was this that put them in the location predicted in the 16th Karmapa's prophecy letter in time to be found by the search party. Apo Gaga prepared himself to leave, packing some things shortly before the advance search party arrived. He awoke early on the morning of the day they came and placed some of his clothes on the back of his goat, a special one without horns, and told his mother that his monks were coming and that he was now ready to leave for his monastery; it would be good if he could take one or two gifts with him from the Kalek monastery! His elder brother, Yeshe Rabsal, who was at Kalek when the advance party arrived, sent word to Apo Gaga to say that monks from Tsurphu were at Katok, on their way to Ba-kor, probably looking for the reincarnation of a special lama. News of this brought great joy to the young Karmapa, who laughed and danced.

Because Apo Gaga was so clear that the monks were seeking him, his parents set up a special tent to receive the visitors. After the traditional politenesses of greeting and exchange of white scarves (*katta*), the advance party enquired after the births of Loga's children and about any dreams she or others in the family may have had. The parents told of their son's birth, the special signs, the dream of the cranes, premonitory dreams his brother and father had had, the cuckoo, the sound of the conch shell, the three suns and so forth. In fact, the advance party had already heard most of this through the discreet enquiries that they had made among the other nomads of the camp. Lama Domo, representing Tsurphu in the advance party, then gave the father a copy of the 16th Karmapa's prediction and Dondrup realised who exactly his son was. After the elated search party had spent some time with Dondrup's astounded family, they accompanied the young Karmapa to Kalek monastery to await the coming of Akong Tulku Rinpoche and Sherab Tarchin, who were expected within days. They soon arrived. Word of the precious discovery was sent back to the Tai Situpa and the Goshir Gyaltsabpa in India, who in turn informed HH the Dalai Lama. When their joyous confirmation of the new Karmapa's identity was received at Kalek monastery, Akong Rinpoche and Sherab Tarchin presented Apo Gaga, now become His Holiness the 17th Gyalwa Karmapa, with the special robes and sacred blessings of the *tru.sol* that they were carrying on behalf of the Tai Situpa and the Goshir Gyaltsabpa and which had been especially prepared in India at the outset of their journey.

As is usual with the discovery of a tulku, offerings were made to the Karmapa's parents to express gratitude for the care that they had given him up to the time of discovery. The initial finding of the Karmapa now completed, a short period was spent in the Kalek area during which Akong Rinpoche made acquaintance with the Karmapa and his family as the full import of what was happening settled in. Preparations were made for the journey to Tsurphu. Akong Rinpoche and Sherab Tarchin, representing the Tai Situpa and the Goshir Gyaltsabpa, and

Tsurphu monastery

a new group of representatives just arrived from Tsurphu, eventually accompanied the Karmapa on his historic journey back to Tsurphu, the seat his former emanation had left some 33 years previously. Before the party left Kalek monastery, three suns appeared in the hazy sky and were seen by many hundreds of people in the surrounding area. The middle one was larger and had a rainbow halo, while the other two were smaller and nestling in the clouds. There could well be a meteorological explanation for such a phenomenon, but even so it would still be what the Tibetans call 'an auspicious coincidence'.

The Karmapa's arrival at Tsurphu was a moving moment for the thousands of Tibetans who had quickly gathered there as news of his coming spread. Descending from his vehicle the Karmapa made the last part of the journey mounted upon a beautifully-apparelled white steed, wearing a special coiffe and accompanied by monks carrying silk banners and playing the traditional musical instruments. Tibetans are famous for their equestrian skills. Many were there on horseback as an escort, dignified in their upright bearing on their small but powerful mounts. The Karmapa entered Tsurphu itself beneath a gigantic golden parasol, a sign of his high rank, to be greeted by a mighty crowd. Descending from his horse with great power of presence for one so young, he was seated in front of the main temple. Dancers in two-man snow-lion costumes performed antics and presented him with 'snow-lion's milk' to drink, and masked representations of the Kagyu protectors came to greet him one by one, as did the figure of an ancient sage, in symbolic wish for his life to be long and healthy.

In general, the days following his arrival were a great celebration for the makeshift city of people who had spontaneously gathered there, with lay folk-dancing, instrumental music and singing. Every day the Karmapa gave his blessing to the vast crowds.

On June 27th, the government of the People's Republic of China officially approved Urgyen Trinley Dorje as the 17th reincarnation of the Karmapa. He who had been, eight hundred years before, the first reincarnate lama of Tibet became the first *tulku* permitted by the Chinese government since 1959. This recognition was undoubtedly aided by the fact that many previous Karmapas were gurus of the Emperors of China.

Meanwhile Tai Situpa and the Goshir Gyaltsabpa were busy with the necessary preparations for the coming enthronement, as well having to deal with the difficulties mentioned in the previous chapter. They visited HH the Dalai Lama who gave them his official sealed certificate confirming the reincarnation, as well as presents for the Karmapa, including his personal *mala* (prayer beads). While they were there, they also received the results of the Tibet State Oracle's vision, confirming HH the Dalai Lama's judgement that Apo Gaga, now Urgyen Trinley Dorje, was the Karmapa. They then sought visas for entry into Tibet to enthrone His Holiness officially and permission was also obtained for a hair-cutting and naming ceremony to be held in Lhasa's famous Jokhang temple, the home of the Jowo, the statue of Buddha Sakyamuni brought to Tibet from China by Princess Wen-Ch'eng in the 7th century. This statue is said to have come to China from India where, some say, it had been made during the Buddha's lifetime by the artist Visvakarman and blessed by Lord Buddha himself. It depicts the Enlightened One at the age of 12 and is believed to bring great blessing to those who see it.

During this period, representatives of Kagyu Buddhism from many nations prepared themselves for a journey to Tibet to attend the enthronement of the teacher for whom they and their numerous organisations worldwide had been waiting so long. After years of uncertainty and anxiety and a distinct feeling of

HH the 17th Karmapa with the 12th Tai Situpa.

being in limbo, the joy of the Karmapa's discovery was as tremendous as one might imagine it to be upon hearing good news awaited for a decade. Now it was also crystal clear that the prediction of the great Nyingmapa visionary, Chojur Lingpa, was being fulfilled and that the Tai Situpa would be the main guru of the new Karmapa. Almost a century previously, Chojur Lingpa had had a vision in which he had seen all the Karmapas up to the twenty-first incarnation. This is how he described the vision concerning the 17th Karmapa:

> *In the area (of the vision) in front of the mountains, (there are) rocks and ancient trees, and there is the seventeenth of the incarnation rosary, together with Khentin Tai Situ, their minds fused as one. This (signifies) that the leaves and petals of the Buddha's teachings will flourish (under him) and there will be abundant fruit of the very essence of the transmissions of Gampopa.*

The Tai Situpa, to whom the previous Karmapa had entrusted the prediction letter, would be as one with the mind of the young Karmapa. This was also what the prediction letter itself had foreseen:

He is sustained by Lord Dönyö Drup.

Pema Dönyö is the name the 16th Karmapa had himself given to the Tai Situ-pa, some thirty years previously. He gave that particular name according to Guru Rinpoche's prophecies in a text called the *Gongdu*, which gave names for the Tai Situpas. This is the tenth of those names. HH the Dalai Lama, in an address he gave on Indian radio to Kagyu followers, also made it clear that the Tai Situpa and the Goshir Gyaltsabpa were the main lamas responsible for finding and installing the 17th Gyalwa Karmapa.

The Tai Situpa and the Goshir Gyaltsabpa arrived in Tibet on July 12. After an overnight stay in the capital, Lhasa, and a visit en route to Pawo Rinpoche's monastery where they conferred blessings on hundreds of pilgrims, they arrived at Tsurphu where they were received with grand ceremony. Tsurphu has been the seat of the previous 16 Karmapas and was founded in 1190 by Karmapa Dusum Chenpa. Until the Cultural Revolution, it housed some nine hundred monks and had four internal monasteries, set within a vast complex of buildings. One of the four monasteries was the seat of the Goshir Gyaltsabpas, who tradi-tionally represent the Karmapas between incarnations — *gyal tshab* means regent.

Recent reconstruction amid the ruins at Tsurphu monastery

Drupon Dechen Rinpoche, the present abbot of Tsurphu, was the former retreat master of Rumtek. He had left Tibet in 1959 with HH the 16th Karmapa, when some of Tsurphu's main relics and holy objects had been carried for safety to Sikkim and stored in the Rumtek treasury. The 16th Karmapa had advised him to return to Tsurphu to supervise its reconstruction. It has indeed risen from its ruins in recent years, thanks to Drupon Dechen Rinpoche and the work of many dedicated people. In particular, Ward Holmes and the Tsurphu Foundation he created have stimulated worldwide interest in this remarkable place. Nestling between huge peaks in the Tolung valley, the walled monastic complex sits next to the beautiful bubbling waters of the river, reminiscent of a powerful Scottish torrent. Geomantically it is a very special site, auspiciously located with respect to the surrounding hills and valleys. The neighbouring mountains are considered sacred locations where the various energies and blessings of the vajrayana mandala are concentrated.

HH the Dalai Lama had advised that everything concerning the enthronement of the Karmapa be done very properly in accordance with spiritual tradition. Thus the first meeting between the Karmapa and the two rinpoches was a formal one. Having been received by the snow lions and masked performers outside the temple, the Tai Situpa and the Gyaltsabpa were shown up to the Karmapa's apartment where they paid their first homage to him and presented him with offerings. In the days which followed they also came to know him in less formal, more playful ways. The delicate, loving and respectful bonds between them were forged very naturally: it was an immaculate meeting between great beings, two of whom will be the future gurus of the third, who himself was the former guru of his new teachers. Emanations of Avalokitesvara, Maitreya and Vajrapani were meeting just as they had so many times in the past and in the scriptures. The Tai Situpa and the Gyaltsabpa discovered, as Akong Rinpoche had been doing for more than a month, the remarkable continuity between the 16th and 17th Karmapas: his fearlessness, assuredness, sense of humour and sincere natural compassion — qualities just like those of his predecessors.

At one point a surprise was prepared for the young Karmapa. During one of the picnics arranged for him in the hills close to Tsurphu, he was led to a marquee where a generator, TV and video player had been set up. He enjoyed watching some films and then his attention was suddenly riveted by footage of his previous incarnation. This striking moment was captured by Clemens Kuby in *Living Buddha*, the documentary film he made on the Karmapa's discovery and enthronement.

The next formal step in the Karmapa's installation would be the ordination known commonly as the 'hair-cutting ceremony'. This was arranged to take place in the holy shrine of the Jokhang temple in Lhasa in the early hours of August 2, 1992. The Tai Situpa and Goshir Gyaltsabpa conducted the religious ceremony before the sacred image representing the Buddha's own presence. It was only the second time that a Karmapa had received this ordination there. Offerings were

*Gyaltsab Rinpoche (right) sprinkling consecrated water on the Karmapa's head
after the hair-cutting by the Tai Situpa (left)*

presented to the Karmapa, including gifts from His Holiness the Dalai Lama: a message for his long life and activity, a blessing scarf and cord and His Holiness's personal prayer beads. Marking their acceptance of the Karmapa reincarnation, representatives of the Lhasa authorities were also present.

After the Karmapa, flanked by the two rinpoches, had made prostration before the Jowo image, and appropriate prayers and mandala offerings had been made, the Tai Situpa cut small strands of his hair, to mark renunciation of worldliness. The Gyaltsabpa sprinkled consecrated water on the place of hair-cutting. The Karmapa then received his incarnation name, inscribed on golden silk and read aloud by the two rinpoches. The name was chosen according to the prophecy of Guru Rinpoche, as found in the discovered treasures (*terma*) of Chogyur Dechen Lingpa. The 17th Gyalwa Karmapa's name is:

*Pal Khyabdak Rangjung Urgyen Gyalway Nyugu Drondul
Trinley Dorje Tsal Chokle Nampar Gyalway De*

Each of these words is charged with dharma significance, worthy of pages of commentary. A simplified meaning would be approximately:

*The Glorious All-Pervading Spontaneously-Manifest (Guru of) Oddiyana,
Shoot of the Victorious Ones, Vajra of Enlightened Activity to Teach Beings,
Accomplished One, Victorious in each and every Direction.*

*The Tai Situpa and the Gyaltsabpa reading the name of the new Karmapa
during the naming ceremony at the Jokhang*

Enthronement

Over 20,000 pilgrims assembled at Tsurphu for the Karmapa's enthronement on September 27, 1992. Besides the main organisations of the Karma Kamtsang tradition worldwide, there were representatives of all the other traditions of Tibetan Buddhism, as well as of the Bön religion, and representatives from the different regions. However, most of the 20,000 were Tibetans, some of whom had made journeys of more than a thousand kilometres to be present. Many tulkus came from all over Tibet and from India and Himalayan areas. For Tibetans, it is considered a very wonderful thing simply to be present at such an occasion, and the chance of just seeing the new Karmapa means more to them than most of us can imagine. This would already have been true before 1959 and was doubly true in 1992 as people's religious faith was reinforced by a ray of hope for the future of Buddhism in their land.

The Tolung valley around Tsurphu became a gigantic and colourful campsite. There were Tibetan girls, and wives wearing bright rainbow aprons, sporting a rich variety of regional hairstyles, ornamented with large turquoises, corals and ambers . People from every quarter of Tibet were present, all wearing costumes specific to their own areas, the Khampa men with bright red or black braids in their hair. The gathering included dance groups and performers. Wearing masks, brocades or just their local costumes, they performed folk dances in front of the temple, often watched by His Holiness from an upper balcony. On the night before enthronement day, it snowed copiously on the nearby sacred mountains. This was taken as a highly auspicious omen.

Around three hundred tulkus and representatives of other monasteries and dharma-centres had also gathered there. Some of the international gathering of Europeans, Americans, South-East Asians and Africans had also brought their own national costumes to wear at the enthronement ceremony. Gifts and offerings for the Karmapa and his monastery had been pouring in with the pilgrims. Many of these were neatly arranged in the temple in an amazing array: dharma objects such as butter-lamp bowls and offering bowls, ritual objects, some of them finely crafted and adorned with noble metals, religious musical instruments, rolls of cloth and brocade, sack of grains and other foodstuffs, tea and many other gifts. All of these were carefully recorded and a list of donors and donations was ceremonially proclaimed aloud in gratitude. All in all, it made for an historic international gathering of great colour and excitement.

The Minister for Religious Affairs, representing the People's Republic of China, presided over the first part of the ceremony, at which officials of the Lhasa authorities were also present. This lasted for some thirty minutes. He announced the official acknowledgement of the Karmapa by the government and gave assurance of his government's intention of supporting religious freedom in China. He presented His Holiness with the written acknowledgement, bearing the State seal. National and regional Chinese TV cameramen were there to record, and later transmit, the event. Despite the obvious political intentions behind this presence, it represented a watershed in policy trends concerning Tibetan Buddhism. One of Tibet's most important religious leaders, who has the full support of HH the Dalai Lama, has been recognised and enthroned in the traditional way. Without doubt the sublime wisdom and foresight of the Karmapa had led him to take rebirth in Tibet for good reason. His vajra mind, that no one can influence or penetrate, will use all its skill in his delicate situation to bring peace and happiness to the people of that land, as well as those of the rest of the world. Karmapa has no boundary.

On the departure of the officials, there was a half-hour pause and the religious ceremony proper commenced. His Holiness took up his seat on the high Tsurphu throne, donning the beautifully-ornate brocade cloak of his station and the small black 'activity' crown. The Tai Situpa and the Goshir Gyaltsabpa were wearing special robes for the occasion, vivid yet subtle in design and colour and made of rare brocade. The temple itself is a dazzling array of colour and ornate decoration — so exotic that in other circumstances it would be garish. But in Tibet's land of bright sunlight, where vivid colour is the norm, and within its feeling of timeless solemnity, the temple gives the impression of noble richness and heightened sensation.

The Tai Situpa opened the ceremony by presenting His Holiness with the sealed recognition letter of HH the Dalai Lama, the prediction letter written by the former Karmapa and the written prediction of Nechung, the State Oracle of Tibet. This was followed by the chanting of offering prayers, during which the Tai Situpa made offerings of purification consisting of the eight auspicious substances, the eight auspicious symbols and representations of the seven attributes of a universal monarch, each of which the Karmapa blessed by his touch, signifying acceptance.

This was followed by religious discourses. Khenpo Zhönu Dawa, the Abbot of Palpung, gave an exposition of the perfection of wisdom. Adi Rinpoche, head of the Drukpa Kagyu in the kingdom of Nangchen, taught on enlightened body, speech, mind, qualities and activity, and Khenpo Lodro of Burkar monastery spoke on the Manjusri prayer. Following these discourses, HE the Goshir Gyaltsabpa explained the five auspicious conditions, after which he made the formal 37 offerings of the mandala, representing all the finest things in the entire universe of gods and humans. The Tai Situpa then came forward and presented the Karmapa with objects symbolising the enlightened body, speech and mind: a Buddha image, a longevity sutra and a stupa. Urgyen Drodul Trinley Dorje was now enthroned as the 17th Gyalwa Karmapa, supreme head of the Karma Kamtsang tradition of Buddhism.

All these events, witnessed by a few hundred special representatives within the temple, were transmitted by a public address system to the tens of thousands listening intently outside. Upon conclusion of the enthronement proper, the members of this crowd joyfully threw their long white, yellow or red offering scarves towards the monastery. These were caught in mid air and passed or thrown on, from hand to hand, all the way up to the monastery where they were piled up. It was a marvellous sight, like spume on the ocean waves: an ocean of devoted offerings making its way spontaneously towards the living Buddha within the temple walls.

Inside, the representatives of monasteries and organisations from both Tibet and other countries were making their offerings. Then His Holiness concluded the enthronement by giving his personal blessing to the crowd, who were now being admitted to the temple. However, it proved impossible to maintain order in the face of the ardent enthusiasm of the thousands trying to crush into the temple space and the blessing was halted temporarily, to be continued the following day. By the time the blessing was adjourned, the seven-year-old Karmapa had spent some five hours on his throne, maintaining great dignity of bearing. The following morning, some 25,000 people filed before him to receive his personal blessing, many of them presenting offerings they had brought from their villages and encampments.

Empowerment

The following day, September 29, Karmapa Urgyen Trinley Dorje gave blessings for several hours on the temple roofdeck, to individuals and groups of visitors. He then conferred his first formal empowerment as the 17th Gyalwa Karmapa.

HH the 17th Karmapa giving the 'standing Chenresig' empowerment

Although assisted by the Tai Situpa and the Gyaltsabpa, he read the main part of the empowerment in clear ringing tones from the balcony windows of an upper storey of the monastery, in sight of the tens of thousands below, his voice relayed by a PA. The empowerment was that of Avalokitesvara (*Chenresig* in Tibetan) the bodhisattva of whom he is seen to be an emanation. This particular empowerment was that of standing red Chenresig, 'he who shakes the world'. Although every action of the Karmapa's life is seen as having significance, this marked the beginning of his enlightened activity as the enthroned Karmapa.

This moving moment was accompanied by many auspicious signs. The sky was bright, with a few patches of cloud, yet a fall of snowflakes, like a rain of flowers, descended. A very exceptional number of birds gathered and circled high in the sky. But most striking was a long straight rainbow which shone in the sky overhead, behind the wheeling birds.

The 17th Karmapa working at his studies, Summer 1995

Education

Although Urgyen Trinley Dorje had received some education while at Kalek monastery, his thorough education as a Karmapa had now to begin. Under the overall guidance of the Tai Situpa and the Gyaltsabpa, and with Drupon Dechen Rinpoche, Abbot of Tsurphu, close at hand, he will have many things to learn. Because he is the Karmapa, many things are second nature to him. Often he simply needs to be told something once or to read through a text once to assimilate it. Sometimes he knows a topic perfectly well before he has been told of it by anyone. He is remarkably bright with a lightning intelligence and spontaneous wit. Nevertheless, he will have to learn all the various aspects of ritual, textual learning, meditation and so forth, just as all the previous Karmapas have done in the past. This sets an example of diligence for all to follow: if even he has to learn all those things in the proper fashion, then so much the more so for ordinary Buddhists!

For the first part of his education he had the assistance of two exceptionally experienced and mature teachers, both formerly in the service of the 16th Karmapa, Omdze Thubten Zangpo and Lama Lodro Sherab. The latter has since returned to Rumtek, where his services are needed. Under the former, the Karmapa has already learnt the skills required in ritual and has passed his Umdze exam. Umdze means Master of Liturgy and includes many aspects of ritual, religious dance and other monastic skills. A layman, Mr Lodro, is also helping with his education. The young Karmapa memorised by heart one essential part of the liturgy – a text more than a hundred pages long — in less than one month, spending only a fraction of the hour of his daily text lesson on it each day.

The 17th Gyalwa Karmapa is an extraordinary being. Much of what is extraordinary cannot be put in print. He has performed many, many acts which we would call miracles. It is not customary in the Kagyu tradition to publicise them, and their main purpose is to teach those present at the time. However, some have been so public that they have become common knowledge. The greatest miracle is the presence of his limitless compassion and enlightened wisdom here on Earth. I would like to conclude this chapter, which is but a glimpse of this remarkable person, with the sincere prayer that his life be long and healthy and that many millions of people all over the world may benefit from this ray of enlightenment sent to us from the sun of buddhahood.

Chapter Seven

Reincarnation, Emanation and the Names of the Karmapa

Buddhists believe in non-ego yet have a doctrine of reincarnation. Isn't this a contradiction? After all, *who* is there to reincarnate if there is no ego?

That is a very good question — especially in the case of 'reincarnate lamas' such as the Karmapa, who are said to have transcended all ego's delusions. Who or what dwells within their physical shell. What is there to reincarnate?

Some simple clues helpful in explaining these fundamental principles of Buddhism will be presented in the pages which follow. Yet one point has to be made. The really satisfactory explanations are to be found not in print but *only* through the direct insight which occurs in the crisp clarity of meditation.

These days one finds some highly readable comments on the rebirth of ordinary people and the reincarnation of lamas. In a laudable effort to make the concepts of Buddhism more readily understandable, modern similes based on physics, psychology, neurology and the like are expertly conjured in zippy language to explain . . . *it happens like this*. But beware! A most essential point is missing in nearly all of them; an understanding of the fundamental nature of reality. Because of this lacuna these descriptions do not ring quite true. They are like a conversation between two people deluded by a mirage, trying to work out where the water has come from and what sort of fish might be found in it; or like the mumblings of someone talking in his sleep, describing the world of his dreams as a vivid reality. In brief, the details are relatively correct within their context but the context itself makes them wrong in an absolute sense. A dreamer may dream of using a ruler to prove that it really *is* a seven-foot-long ant he is riding and, in the dream, he might feel triumphantly proven right; only to awaken to realise that all was not quite as he had thought!

Beyond the light-heartedness of these examples, it is extremely important to know that ordinary reason cannot explain everything and that some things are true mysteries. 'Mystery' usually means one of two things in a religion: a cover-up for a flaw in its logic or something that is truly too subtle for the mind to understand from its present perspective.

Buddhist teachings make it clear that it is not until one has reached the eighth level of voidness — the eighth bodhisattva level where every intellectual preconception and all subject-object perception is transcended — that the real truth of these matters emerges. This means that every matter-of-fact, intellectual explanation of rebirth or causality is only good, at best, as a stopgap measure; a crutch to help one along the path.

Something refreshing in the Kagyu teachings reawakens a sense of wonder in life, a freshness in perception. It shakes off the stale yet stubborn attempts of the intellect to reduce everything to that which can be explained in terms of familiar reference points. It is said that a man in Belfast was asked whether he was Catholic or Protestant and replied, "I'm a Buddhist", to which the reply came, "Yes, but a Catholic Buddhist or a Protestant Buddhist?"

The ineffable, unimaginable nature of all existence, including reincarnation, need not be viewed in disappointment but in welcome relief. As Bengar Jampal Zangpo, the sixth Karmapa's great disciple said of true open-mindedness:

> . . . *bless the true meditator who can realise the freshness of the instant,*
> *without speculation or contrivance, just being in it, as it is . . .*

Relative and ultimate truths

One very useful key opens many doors to Buddhism and its tenets. It is the distinction between what is relatively true and what is ultimately true. Some Buddhist ideas (such as reincarnation) are attempts at explaining the mechanisms of what happens on the *seemingly true* level of reality — the relatively true world of our mental imagery; the personal movie we are living out; a subjective, interpretative landscape based on thoughts, memories and the various stories we constantly tell ourselves to explain life. The mind experiencing this world is like a camera constantly set on zoom, totally absorbed in its focus.

Other areas of Buddhism (such as non-ego) point us towards the *really true*, an ultimately true, non-subjective reality far greater in its scope and depth than our limited conceptual pictures. This could be compared to a wide-angle shot: the image is clear and sharp but is set within a panorama with lots of space.

When we explain things to children, we need to enter into their world and use imagery that is familiar to them. What we tell them has to prove true within their own terms of reference. Without lying, we just formulate the very best truth available, according to the world-picture in the mind of the young listener. The Buddha's relative truth teachings — about karma, reincarnation, suffering, impermanence and so forth — are all relatively-true teachings, geared to the actual experience of the worldly mind. They act as stepping stones towards something higher, just as better and better mathematical models succeed one another as we work our way through school and on to university. Buddhism is not a simple, single set of ideas. It has many levels of language suited to different audiences and various levels of teachings suited to different maturities of being.

Teachings on ultimate truth — mainly those on non-ego and voidness — are aimed at those already mature in life's wisdom, rich in meditation experience and with a fine intellectual grasp of philosophy. Even then, they are only relatively-ultimate truths, for the real ultimate truth can only shine in a mind that is totally liberated and wise: the mind of a Buddha.

It is important not to mix up the relative and absolute teachings of Buddhism, and to use them appropriately, just as it is important not to baby-talk with grown-ups or to use thesis terminology with a three-year-old.

Reincarnation or emanation?

For his disciples, the Karmapa is the presence of the limitless ultimate within their limited, relative world. He is not a reincarnation in the sense of being a worldly person who died and entered a subsequent life, but rather in the sense of ultimate truth manifesting over and over again *in carne*, in the form of a very precious human being that other human beings can see and hear. Therefore any meeting with the Karmapa is seen, by his followers, as a very special moment — a window to the ultimate. Because of the power of such moments, they believe that the very acts of *hearing, seeing, touching or thinking about* the Karmapa can speed one towards liberation. Although the word 'incarnate' can be explained this way, it would be more appropriate to call the Karmapa an *emanation*, as this fits in clearly with the theory of mahayana Buddhism and gives an image of a radiance from some central purity. This is more accurate than the notion of someone who is simply the reincarnation of someone else.

Both Buddhas and bodhisattvas have the power to emanate in compassionate, spontaneous response to the need of beings. To say *emanate at will* would not be quite right because the notion of will is very much to do with ego and theistic concepts, which relate human will and divine will. Some writers' accounts of the after-death experience of reincarnate lamas make them sound like aeroplane pilots skilfully, wilfully guiding their craft on to the next airfield. In such cases the ideas of guiding will and intentional control are the writer's own transposition based on a theist mind-set.

Such a notion of will is almost the antithesis of that of a spontaneous play of natural goodness, radiating from a mind freed from ego-delusions. In texts such as *The Changeless Nature*, we find it clearly explained that will and thought are not necessary for perfect emanation into other people's worlds. The sun does not need to plan its radiance into each and every flower or to will itself to shine on them. Monsoon rainfalls do not need to remember to fill each river or to try to make the peafowl shriek. In nine excellent examples, Maitreya, the Changeless Nature's true author, shows things which take place spontaneously, by their very nature, without thought, will or effort. After the nine he explains that no example from our world can adequately portray enlightened activity; it is not quite like anything we have ever known. In an earlier chapter, he concludes:

> *That which is beyond birth, suffering and death*
> *manifests as being born, suffering and dying,*
> *in order to bring help to beings . . . this is truly wondrous.*

Reincarnation of ordinary people

Buddhist reincarnation theory deals with life in the *seems to be* world: people being born and growing up, some rich, some poor, some gifted, some deprived — the whole panoply of human (and other) situations, some seemingly unfair and some fortunate beyond most people's wildest dreams. Most of our world's belief systems have had to tackle the knotty problem of explaining, in terms of their own framework of ideas, life's horrors and sufferings as well as its joys. Theists speak of God's purpose, some atheists of biological accident, and so on and so forth. The Buddha taught that causes naturally produce their effects. Just as what we did early on in this life was crucial in shaping what followed in later years, so likewise what we did in former existences helped shape this life as a whole. And what we are doing in this life is gradually shaping the future ones. The quality of both what happens to us and how it affects us is seen as the natural fruition of past actions.

The creation of the future, through actions, takes place according to natural laws of cause and effect which have an inbuilt morality. Good produces happiness. Harm produces suffering. It simply happens just like that. These laws work infallibly and without any external 'law-enforcement agency', just as gravity works naturally. When we throw a ball up into the air, we do not expect some external being to catch it, measure its velocity and throw it back down to earth accordingly. It falls by the very nature of things. Likewise, Buddhists see acts of basic goodness as naturally bringing well-being back to the doer, and harmful acts as bringing suffering, in the long term, without there being any external arbiters who reward or punish. This happens through the very nature of mind and through the interdependence of everything.

Whereas it is totally unimportant to know whether or not we were formerly Christopher Columbus or Sarah Bernhardt, it is extremely useful to understand that if we are rich now, it is perhaps because of being generous in the past, and that if we have poor health now, maybe we harmed the health and life of others in former times. Innate tendencies of all sorts — to intelligence, to anger, to violence, to intense loneliness, to constant dissatisfaction, or to compassion, generosity, care for others and so forth — can also all be the inheritance of former lives. Besides this sort of conditioning shaping mental tendencies, there are also specific causes which will at one time or another produce specific effects, like seeds sown in the past which will burgeon only at some particular time in the future when the 'climate', the circumstances of the time in terms of people and places, is just right.

The general theory is that any deed motivated by selfishness, desire, anger, jealousy, pride or the like will produce suffering for its doer in some future time. Conversely, any deed motivated by impartial love, compassion, wisdom and the like will produce happiness for the doer. The complex details of what various physical, verbal and mental actions can programme into the doer's future are discussed in the Buddhist teachings on karma, which, as we have seen, means action.

A garden is a useful example of a complex of processes of cause and effect. The trees exist over a timespan of hundreds of years, bushes for decades, some flowering plants for a few years, some mushrooms for only a few days. All together, these various elements make the garden. There are reasons for each plant being how it is — the seed it came from, the soil it grows in and the treatment it has received. Second by second, within each plant, one micro-biological moment is creating the next. Just during one day within one plant, there may be a myriad-fold evolution of chemical and cellular events. What takes place in the whole garden from day to day is inconceivable. Yet, seen from afar, it just seems like one fairly static thing: 'the garden'. Human beings are similar. Each ongoing reality in a human mind has its own cause-and-effect chaining; in the body too. What happens in them all in one day is inconceivable. Within that complexity, it is always the case that past causes are responsible for present effects. That present effect in turn becomes a new cause: the creation ground of the future.

After death, the imprints etched into consciousness while alive remain present deep within the mind, to become, at the time of future conception, the consciousness equivalent to the genetic data provided by the parents' sperm and ovum. Just as the future hair colour and physical features are already programmed in the genes, so is the ground for the future mentality already programmed in the mind that arrives from a former life. Through the successive traumas of death, the post-death experience and nine months spent as an embryo and then a foetus in the womb, the superficial persona of the past life is all but erased while the powerful inner tendencies of mind and an incredible amount of latent programming remains. Just as a predisposition to Alzheimer's disease in old age may be present in the new-born baby's body, so are future affective — and many other — predispositions already present in the mind.

Another being is born. One life leads on to another. The power of the ongoing force of past actions makes continuous reincarnation inevitable, as surely as today's heavy rain makes tomorrow's swelling of the river inevitable. As long as there is illusion, we go on and on, from life to life. According to whether illusions and actions are mainly positive or negative, the quality of life goes up or down, but reincarnation never stops. One has no choice in the matter.

Karmapas and reincarnation

This is the ordinary meaning of reincarnation and in those terms the Karmapa is viewed as being *not even in one atom's-worth a reincarnated human being* (Thrangu Rinpoche). To be that, he would need to be under the sway of illusion; the driving force behind his presence in this world would have to be worldly karma, and this is not the case.

The Karmapa is viewed as being a bodhisattva of the highest (tenth) level; the one at the threshold of total enlightenment. To attain even the first bodhisattva level, one has to be totally free of karma that creates rebirth. Having burst free from the fetters of illusion, constantly seeing the ultimate truth and filled with wisdom, the very heart of which is compassion, first-level bodhisattvas will never *have to* be reborn. Any manifestation they might have in the world is through choice and its motive forces are innate compassion and the power of connection with other beings, whom they come to help. This is very different from a motive force of delusion, self-interest and karma.

The first bodhisattva level, known as 'Joy Supreme', represents a tremendous breakthrough point. In many scriptures it is already called enlightenment, even though there are nine, long-enduring levels to traverse before a Buddha's enlightenment is reached. It is said that, despite their wisdom, first-level bodhisattvas cannot even begin to imagine what the experience of second-level bodhisattvas is like, and so on. On the tenth level, the bodhisattva's compassionate radiance in the lives of beings is described as being no different from that of the Buddhas. Only the inner realisation is different.

The Karmapa, now at the apex of bodhisattva maturity on this tenth level, is predicted to become the sixth Buddha of this age; an age, in this sense, being the lifespan of our solar system. Sakyamuni, the 'Sage of the Sakyas', two-and-a-half thousand years ago in India, was the fourth Buddha. In thousands of years from now, Maitreya, 'Loving Kindness' Buddha will be the fifth and then he who is presently the Karmapa will be Buddha Simha, 'the Lion Buddha'. In the Good Age Sutra, just over one thousand Buddhas are predicted to come and teach here before our world is consumed by cosmic fire. Could this be the sun's expansion that physicists expect in millions of years' time?

The Karmapa is said to exist on such a level of purity that when acting for the Buddhas, he is indistinguishable from them. Furthermore, as with the Buddha, there is one Karmapa for every being in our galaxy. For this reason, a popular way of interpreting the meaning of the name Karmapa is not only as 'The One of (Buddha) Activity' but also as 'The Star One', as the Tibetan word for star sounds like the word for action, only the spelling being slightly different (*skar.ma* as opposed to *ka.rma*).

In the bodhisattva scriptures it says that the mind of a first-level bodhisattva is so clear, so free and so pure that, in one instant of meditation, it can experience simultaneously one hundred different Buddhas and receive various teachings from each of them. Furthermore, in one instant, it can radiate into the lives of up to one hundred different persons, helping them in a suitable way. Like this, there are twelve different abilities, each a hundredfold. As the bodhisattva level changes, so the amplitude of those twelve activities increases, reaching unimaginable proportions. For this reason, one cannot think of a tenth-level bodhisattva such as the Karmapa as simply being one person in one place, who dies and then reappears somewhere else. It is more the case that one minute fraction — like one

The 17th Karmapa viewing video footage of his predecessor

twinkle from a diamond — is perceived in one circumstance and another facet in a different circumstance, according to those who perceive it. The diamond has endless possibilities of twinkling.

Those who knew the previous Karmapa bore witness to this. He was perfect in every situation and transformed from second to second according to the circumstances; unbelievably kind when it was needed, powerful if that was required and wrathful if that was the best thing to be. This happened immediately and effortlessly, just as a mirror effortlessly reflects with minute precision whatever passes in front of it. Like the diamond, like the mirror, the Karmapa is indescribable. Each person experiences his or her own version of him and for that reason there is a Karmapa for everyone. Whatever colours and patterns one sees in the diamond, the gem itself is always magnificent and pure. Whatever image is seen in the mirror is always perfectly tailored to the one who is looking. However one experiences the Karmapa, it is directly relevant to one's own life.

One important distinction must be made however. Although there are limitless Karmapa emanations, many appearing simultaneously and some even mentioned by the Karmapas themselves, there is only one Gyalwa Karmapa who is the enthroned head of the Karma Kagyu Buddhist tradition. Of this there is no doubt.

Some times, some situations, some geographical locations are more powerful than others. One key moment spent in a certain place can shape what will happen for years to come. According to Tibetan astrology and Buddhist teachings on karma, times and places can catalyse the power of actions, multiplying it a hundred- or a thousandfold. To be in the presence of holy persons is one such catalyst and, for Kagyu Buddhists, being in the presence of the Karmapa is something very special. In the past, Tibetans would prostrate their way over hundreds of kilometres, sometimes for months on end, on pilgrimage to holy places or great people. Doubtless the psychological investment they put into their goal gave a lifelong significance to the final experience, when it came. The intense purification of their minds by incessant prayer during the pilgrimage created fertile terrain for what they received at its end. All in all, such pilgrimages were a marvellous meeting of the ability to bless and the openness to receive blessing.

In particular, the power of wishes, or prayers, made in the Karmapa's presence are said to have tremendous power — enough, if one is deeply sincere, to influence many lives to come. This is explained through the power of interdependence. For this reason, the Karmapa is also known as *Yi.Shin.Nor.Bu*, the Wish-Fulfilling Jewel.

Where ultimate and relative meet

When I watch a rainbow on a brilliant but showery summer day, it looks just as though the colours are in a precise place in the sky. But you see them in another place and someone else in yet another position, while a person standing a hundred metres away may see nothing at all. There are no colours 'up there', otherwise we would all see them in the same place. It is an intriguing question to ask oneself where indeed the colours are. The conjuncture of light, water vapour, eye, brain and geographical location gives us each our experience which looks, for all the world, as though it has its real existence outside of ourselves. Afterwards, we can chat around the evening fireside about the lovely rainbow we *all* saw. Really we are talking about many parallel subjective experiences.

The relative-truth teachings of Buddhism go into details about the way our subjective experiences create themselves. That *seems to be* world is our lives. In it, we each live out a personal dream, convinced of the reality of our own picture of things. Resentful people see the world as a vicious, unfair place. Romantics see it as wonderful. Physicists see it as atoms, artists as a mass of shapes and colours, and sharp businessmen as a way of making bucks.

The ultimate truth teachings are not something other than the above, rather its complement. They have to be. For them to be *ultimate*, there has to be something limited and relative of which they are the ultimate. Likewise, for things to be *relative*, they have to be relative to some absolute. Relative and absolute are two sides of a coin; they exist because of each other. In the absolute truth, which is great wisdom, the *seems to be* reality has no true substance. It is like the wise scientist who understands why he is seeing a rainbow in the sky. The fact that he understands how a rainbow image is formed in a human brain does not switch off the actual experience. It complements it with wisdom that understands at one and the same time what seems to be and what really is. The Buddhist teachings on no-self, non-ego, show the truth behind our projections of personality. Without the projection, there could be no truth. This is why reincarnation theory and non-ego go hand-in-hand. To all intents and purposes, it seems as though we go from day to day, from life to life. But in reality it is a constant transformation, in which all the components of one instant's reality generate the next. Life is a constantly changing continuum.

Within that continuum, the Buddhas, the Karmapas and other great teachers represent the constant light of absolute truth within the relative play of our individual and collective experience: one sun yet a myriad-fold play of colours and shadow.

Chapter Eight

The Samadhirajasutra

". . . knowing this one thing, liberates everything . . ."

Buddha Sakyamuni taught many things to many different sorts of people. During 45 itinerant years of teaching, his audience ranged from simple farmers and traders to philosophers, yogins, princes and ministers, as well as his own dedicated followers. His teachings were a response to the needs, questions and challenges of all these very different sorts of people. The vast body of scriptures which records those teachings fills more than a hundred volumes.

India at that time was a great hub of true civilisation — the peoples of its many kingdoms loved philosophy and religion. It was an age of great thinkers; those whose ideas have marked the world's philosophy ever since. In the two centuries that followed the Buddha, Confucius appeared in China and Plato and Aristotle in Greece. In India they set their mind to contemplating such things as the existence and nature of the smallest building blocks of the universe, resorting to notions such as differential calculus in trying to work out the spatial relationships of the very tiniest particles. They also debated the relationship between consciousness and matter. *Plus ça change . . .*

In one way, it is astounding to realise that this was happening while Europeans were still living on a relatively tribal basis. But one should not be surprised; after all, the most powerful scientific instrument of all time is the human mind, its intelligence and intuition often penetrating the truth long before confirmation by complex technological paraphernalia. Although under normal circumstances technology advances from century to century, the quality of human intelligence, compassion, harmony and civility does not. It is a mistake of vanity to assume automatically that our thinking is more advanced than that of the past.

In particular, India was a land of intense spirituality where meditation was commonplace. Many people spent the greater part of their lives in the practice of yoga or concentration and Lord Buddha himself studied under the two most reputed contemporary masters of concentration meditation, Alara Kalama and Uddaka Ramaputta — although he soon matched or surpassed them. The former made him his equal and the latter wanted to become his disciple. The Buddha's own account of their meeting is found in the Mahasaccakasutra. What is interesting for us is that he gave his post-enlightenment meditation teachings at such a time and place in the world's history, when meditation was flourishing and his teachings had to vie with many other lines of thought and technique to prove their worth.

Among his many teachings on meditation, the Buddha gave one very special discourse (sutra) towards the end of his life, putting all the various advice he had given into a single perspective. It is called the 'Discourse on the King of Meditative Absorptions' — the samadhirajasutra.

It seems that when the Buddha taught, not only did his speech, with its sixty magnificent qualities, communicate clearly with the intellect of his audience but also his presence enabled many of them — those who were open enough — actually to experience directly something of the inner truth of what he was describing. In the samadhirajasutra he not only explained but showed the one 'Rome' to which all meditation roads lead. Gathered around him at that time were many of his most gifted bodhisattva disciples, as well as, so it is said, a celestial assembly of bodhisattvas and gods. His teaching uplifted many of those present into a lucidity of mind from which they could glimpse the perfectly clear and enlightened mind that he himself had achieved. It was a precious moment revealing the whole purpose of his teaching on Earth.

One key figure in this gripping story was a bodhisattva called 'Moonbeam Youth', Candraprabhakumara. When the Buddha asked the assembly who would be prepared to manifest in later ages to ensure that this vital meaning of his teaching stayed alive, Candraprabhakumara was the natural candidate for the task, which he gladly accepted. Instantly, many other bodhisattvas volunteered to manifest at his side, in future ages and places, to guarantee that this truth of truths remained in the world for as long as possible. This is understood as being the birth of the Kagyu tradition, as fifteen centuries later Candraprabhakumara was to become Gampopa, the great father of the Kagyu, while the other major bodhisattvas were to become the Karmapas and the other holders of the Kagyu lineage who would maintain the teaching through the ages.

In the samadhirajasutra and the mahakarunapundarikasutra, Buddha Sakyamuni predicts the reappearance of Candraprabhakumara as a physician who would serve his teachings. He also predicts the coming of 'the one of enlightened activity' — the Karmapa. The Karmapa's name is founded in this identification.

Within the vast cosmic picture of mahayana Buddhism Candraprabhakumara is seen as someone who had previously manifested in thousands of universes alongside the Buddhas. He is the recurring right-hand-man who labours with purity and diligence to establish the teachings of those Buddhas. This is the inner sense of his name. He remains 'youthful' because he does not pass into enlightenment but remains on the tenth level of bodhisattva development, in order to help others.

The power accumulated in all those ages of service enabled him, when he manifested as Gampopa in the 11th century, to firmly establish the Kagyu lineage, which was already securely in existence although in a small-scale, hermetic way. At that time he enriched the lineage by integrating into it the strengths of the various elements he embodied in his own life: the yogic teachings of his own teacher Milarepa, the excellent Buddhist knowledge he had acquired under the

Khadampas ('Purists') and the Buddhist monastic tradition. Together, these constituted a very complete form of Buddhism. Gampopa's uplifting life story can be found in *The Hundred Thousand Songs of Milarepa*. An ideal and learned monk, beloved of his companions, he could sit comfortably in unwavering meditation for a week, without moving, even quite early on in his life. Then, through meeting Milarepa, he received and perfected the teachings of enlightenment. Such was the guru of the first Karmapa.

That the Kagyu tradition, brought from India to Tibet by Marpa the Translator in the 1070s and 1080s, should be thus augmented is not surprising. It had been predicted by Marpa's own guru Naropa as something that would happen again and again, taking the lineage from strength to strength, as we shall see in the following chapters.

Chapter Nine

'Ka-gyu' — Transmission of Mastery
The Inheritance from Tilopa

Mahayana Buddhism considers that Sakyamuni had already achieved enlightenment before being born as Prince Gautama in Lumbini over 2,500 years ago. It sees his life here on Earth as being but one fraction of that enlightenment's consequences, a necessary drama played out in twelve acts, each of which, including his 'attaining enlightenment' in our eyes, had a vital role to play in his bringing the timeless message of universal truth to our world.

Every one of the twelve stages helped in the proper establishment of his teaching for millennia to come and each had something to contribute to the invigoration he brought to our planet. The coming of a teaching Buddha coincides with a key moment in the destiny of the world and in the complex cycle of reincarnations of its inhabitants. Enacting the twelve deeds is the way in which each of the 1,002 teaching Buddhas who visit our Earth before it is finally burnt up by the sun, will reset in motion the wheel of truth. The noble, exemplary life which they enact at such a time is known as the supreme emanation — supreme nirmanakaya.

The twelve stages are:

— to leave the heavens and manifest on Earth at the most appropriate time
— to enter the womb of a mother so as to be born in the most appropriate family for what will follow
— to be born miraculously
— to grow up showing unique physical prowess and mental intelligence
— to enjoy consorts and the finest pleasures that worldly life can offer
— to leave worldliness
— to practise asceticism more radically than anyone else ever has and then renounce it for its inadequacy
— to go to the place where all the Buddhas of this world manifest enlightenment
— there to vanquish the negative energies of the world
— to show recognition of the Middle Way and attain enlightenment,
— to teach the universal truths and
— to enter nirvana.

Had Gautama not been a rich and handsome prince, not had more beautiful wives than all other men, not been a better athlete and scholar and so forth, how could he be credible later as Gautama Buddha, declaring that worldly possessions are not everything? Had he just been a poor yogi, many might have accused him of sour grapes about worldly pleasures he had never known. Likewise, how could he have convinced people of the non-necessity of self-mortification had he himself not gone without food, sat in the burning Indian midday sun without drinking and so forth, to a degree unsurpassed by anyone else. There is great significance in each aspect of a Buddha's life. It is not just the final and perfect life of a being who has been working from purity to purity through hundreds of lives but the perfect teaching drama; a template for an age to come, a reference point by which all else can be measured.

The supreme nirmanakaya of the Buddha graced the world for 84 years. Yet throughout the five-thousand-year age illuminated by his enlightenment, he remains constantly present in other forms, teaching those whose minds are pure enough and open enough to be aware of them. These can be emanations, nirmanakaya other than the supreme one, appearing, from time to time, in an infinite variety of ways, animate or inanimate, to help human and other beings.

Beyond these there is a constant teaching presence which is so pure and powerfully direct that only experienced bodhisattvas who have reached the ten levels have the subtlety and strength of mind to be aware of it. Called the *sambhogakaya*, it is a state of mental transfiguration no longer sullied by the confusion of worldly ignorance. In that state, every sight and sound is charged with deep and joyous meaning. Its experience consists of thousands of interfaces, each perfect and meaningful, with the overall universal wisdom of enlightenment. These are known as pure lands; pure experience. Although buddhahood and its wisdom can never be realised *directly* for what it is until one attains complete enlightenment and actually becomes it, bodhisattvas experience it *indirectly* through the doors of their mind and senses, as visionary states of insight. Far removed from suffering, yet emanating to help those still suffering, deeply rooted in peace and wisdom, nurtured by this ever-growing vision of perfection, they enjoy the finest access to enlightenment. The term sambhogakaya itself means complete access, complete enjoyment.

Besides the lineages of teaching which stem from the time of the supreme nirmanakaya of Sakyamuni twenty-five centuries ago in India, there are some which stem from his sambhogakaya, as experienced by enlightened bodhisattva teachers down the ages. This enables the buddha mind to bring teachings to the world as and when necessary, to match its changing needs.

Tilopa was one such enlightened bodhisattva. Having gathered together and penetrated the meaning of the teachings of more than one hundred of the most advanced Buddhist gurus of his day, he gained total enlightenment and became inseparable from the buddha mind, uttering at that time the famous couplet:

> "I, Tilo, have no human guru,
> My guru is the mighty Buddha Vajradhara."

Buddha Vajradhara is the aspect of enlightenment from which flow the teachings of vajrayana.

1st page *HH the 17th Gyalwa Karmapa, Urgyen Trinley Dorje, wearing the bodhisattva crown, 1992*
2nd page *HH the 16th Gyalwa Karmapa, Rangjung Rikpe Dorje, wearing the Gampopa crown*
3rd page *'Rainbow body' photo of the 16th Gyalwa Karmapa, Rumtek 1980*
4th page & 5th page top *The arrival of the 17th Karmapa at Tsurphu monastery in Central Tibet, June 1992*
5th page lower *The visionary lama instrumental in the early years of the Karmapa's life, Abbot Amdo Palden of Kalek monastery*
6th page *HH the 17th Karmapa in the arms of Akong Tulku Rinpoche, the Tai Situpa's representative in the search party*
7th page *HH the 17th Karmapa with the Goshir Gyaltsabpa (left), 1992*
Above *HH the 17th Karmapa with the Tai Situpa (right)*

The Tai Situpa making offering to the Karmapa during the enthronement ceremony, September 1992

Above and opposite *HH the 17th Gyalwa Karmapa, Urgyen Trinley Dorje, wearing the bodhisattva crown, 1992*

HH the 17th Karmapa wearing a mahapandita's hat

HH the 17th Karmapa wearing the Gampopa crown

Above and opposite *HH the 17th Karmapa, Tsurphu, Summer 1995*
Final page *His Holiness's little brother, 'Rinpoche', with Apo Gaga after his recognition as the 17th Karmapa*

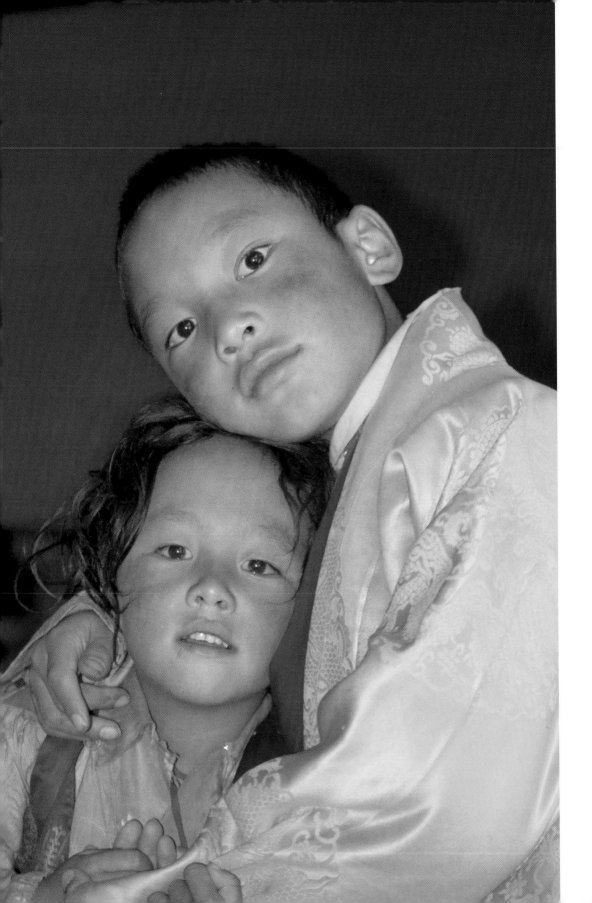

Tilopa

Indian Buddhist biographies were probably a rich oral tradition while Buddhism was widespread in India. It was not unusual in those days for people to carry their knowledge in the heart and mind, committing volumes to memory. Many abbots were able to recite by heart more than half the hundred volumes of the Buddha's recorded teachings. Some even knew them all. Unfortunately the demise of Buddhism in India destroyed its oral traditions. What remains is very little, preserved thanks to  the writings, and their subsequent printing, of biographers from other countries, especially Tibetans — a people with a very systematic mentality, rather different from the romantic and beautifully complicated Indian mind which, as its architecture and music betray, delights in obtuse diversion and the non-concrete.

Tilopa occurs twice among the famous 84 mahasiddhas of Indian Buddhism — as Tilopa and Tillipa, although some believe that these were two separate individuals. The following summary is based upon the present Tai Situpa's biography of Tilopa, for which he drew upon the various fragments of biography which have survived the ages.

There is an interesting parallel between the conception of Tilopa and that of the present Karmapa. In both cases, the parents turned to a holy man in their attempts to secure the child they wanted, had their wishes fulfilled by the birth of a son, born amid unusual signs, and then found they were the parents of a wonder child whose life, even from an early age, was to be guided by the greatest spiritual teachers of his time.

In Tilopa's case, the guidance came from the commanding appearance of a dakini, who manifested at important moments in his life to point him in the right direction. From the very outset, she made it clear to him that his real parents were not his worldly ones, but rather primordial wisdom and universal voidness:

". . . your father is Cakrasamvara and your mother is Vajravarahi."

On her advice, he frequented monasteries and gradually took up a monk's life, eventually becoming an erudite scholar and an exemplary monk, known as Prajnabhadra. Following a vision he discovered a text hidden in the base of a statue in the monastery. Not understanding its meaning he prayed to his dakini mentor, who sent him to the illustrious gurus Matangi and Saryapa to study tantra. Returning some time later to the monastery, he furthered his classical studies. Another critical encounter with his celestial dakini teacher initiated him further and definitively closed the gaps that existed between his theoretical knowledge and his experiential insight.

Following this he travelled widely in India, going from guru to guru until he had assimilated the very quintessence of each major strand of vajrayana teaching of the day. In particular he received from Saryapa the teachings on purification of chakra and subtle body, best known these days through their Tibetan name of *tummo*. From Nagarjuna he received the illusory body and radiant light teachings; from Lawapa the dream yoga; from Sukhasiddhi the teachings on life, death and between-life states (bardo) and consciousness transference; from Indrabhuti teachings on insight (prajna) as the balancing of energies and from Matangi the teachings on resurrection of the dead body. Understanding the many parallels he found in the various traditions, and realising that they each responded to the needs of different people at different stages of awakening, he eventually condensed their essence into four principal streams of teaching. It is from these, and in these, that we have the true meaning of the word Kagyu. In Tai Situpa's words: "Taking advantage of his new-found freedom, Prajnabhadra practised meditation very intensively, travelling when necessary to receive the special techniques and guidance of most of the great teachers of his day: Guhya, Darika, Dingi and so on. The best of students, he mastered all their vital teachings and was able to appreciate their common points and their particularities. The lineages which he inherited all condense into four streams of transmitted wisdom. It is from these that the Kagyu tradition derives its name, for 'Kagyu' is a short form of the Tibetan *theg pa gsum gy snying don* **bka** *bab kyi chos bzhi'i gdams ngag bar ma ckad pa'i* **brgyud** *pa*, which roughly means *the unbroken* **lineage** *of profound and intimate guidance in the four sorts of* **transmitted mastery***, the heart meaning of the three yanas.*

"In the above, Ka is short for *Ka pap zhi* — which could be loosely rendered as 'four transmissions of mastery'. *Zhi* simply means four. *Ka pap* is a term without any equivalent in English. It means transmission — of knowledge, skill, insight and teaching ability — in a specific domain, from master to student, to the point where the student enters into complete possession of all the master's prowess. It is the sort of thing that takes place when someone already gifted in, or deeply predisposed towards, a certain subject seeks out the best person in that field and learns from them everything they have to teach. Implicit to this process is the spontaneous appreciation and rapid assimilation that occurs when a student has a natural feel for a subject.

"The four Kagyu transmissions referred to here are those of:

1. great seal — (Tib. *phyag.rgya.cken.po* Skt. *mahamudra*) in this instance 'uncharacterised mahamudra', i.e. without ritual, form or sophistry
2. heat yoga — (Tib. *gtum.mo,* which literally means 'angry mother')
3. lucidity — (Tib. *od.gsal* means 'as clear as if illuminated' — sometimes called 'clear light' in modern translations) this includes dream and between-life *(bardo)* yogas
4. union — (Tib. *las.kyi.phyag.rgya,* Skt. karma mudra)

"... These four transmissions contain the very essence of all three levels (yana) of Buddhism. Each contains the others and therefore each contains everything. As a whole they are called mahamudra.

"If each of the above were not an aspect of a whole, *tummo*, subtle heat, would simply be a technique for producing warmth; one would be no more than a human oven. Radiant lucidity would be just something illuminating, like torchlight. They are not like that. Subtle heat and lucidity are very profound practices, richly supported by mahamudra's insight, mantras, visualisation-stage mahamudra etc. They are very complete, each being a highlighted aspect of the same thing.

"These four, one of which is intimate knowledge of mind and the other three skilful areas of technique, have been transmitted in their original integrity, via a lineage of perfect masters and perfected students, from the time of Tilopa until our present day. They form the hub of the present Kagyu Lineage."

During this period of his life, Prajnabhadra acquired the name Tilopa, which means 'sesame-grinder', as this was the external guise in which he lived, while all the time perfecting his meditation internally. A marvellous phrase occurs in this part of his biography:

"From this moment on, not one moment of his life, day or night, was wasted."

Having inherited the Buddhist lineages of his time, Tilopa was then advised by his guiding dakini to go to the impenetrable valleys of Orgyen, where he would receive extraordinary transmissions of teaching. In a spiritual journey of epic proportions, worthy of the most vivid fairy tale, he made his way through earthquakes, hallucinations, demon army attacks and other phenomena and was rewarded by becoming heir to some very special teachings: the heart teachings of the dakinis. These included the nine secret dakini teachings and the four wish-fulfilling-gem teachings.

Then followed his enlightenment. Although he had had many excellent gurus, including celestial dakinis, his enlightenment occurred through direct fusion with the mind of Sakyamuni's sambhogakaya. Tilopa experienced this as meeting 'The Buddha Who Holds the Vajra(yana)' (Vajradhara Buddha). The fivefold transmission of insight that followed is indescribable. It ended with Tilopa being indistinguishable from the enlightenment of all the Buddhas. The remainder of his earthly life was spent teaching and ensuring that the precious wisdom and lineages he had inherited were perpetuated by worthy disciples for the future benefit of humankind. This tremendous spiritual wealth is the first foundation stone of the Kagyu tradition and a major part of what the present Karmapa will formally re-inherit from his principal teacher, the Tai Situpa, and other gurus.

Chapter Ten

Vajrayana

Vajrayana is probably the form of Buddhism least understood by the general public. And the most misunderstood. In temples, dharma centres and books, one can see its vivid, symbolic imagery — sometimes wrathful, sometimes erotic — and truly wonder what its role could be in a faith famous for its peacefulness and disillusion with worldly desire. Those who have such a first reaction to Tibetan Buddhism could be compared to children visiting a hospital for the first time, unaware of the need for medicine and startled by the masks, gowns and needles: objects of fear. Unlike children, experienced doctors appreciate the use of such things which, for them, represent neither fear nor danger but safety. In a surgeon's skilful hands, a razor-sharp blade becomes an ultimate tool of healing. Likewise, once transmuted in the skilful hands of vajrayana practice, the energies of anger, sexuality and so forth become the finest remedies for the aggression and passions which spoil the world. Vajrayana Buddhism does not lead to a different enlightenment than that achieved through the compassionate, easily-explicable path of mahayana Buddhism but it does lead to it infinitely more quickly.

There are two main barriers between the ordinary human mind and enlightenment: one is the habit of self-centred thinking and the other is ignorance of the perfection buried deep within each of us. Mahayana Buddhism is a very skilful way of gradually demolishing these; a well-programmed *path* of mental transformation which, over many hundreds of lifetimes, will lead one to buddhahood. The vajrayana methods gathered by Tilopa, however, are a set of powerful psychological tools which enable those same changes to take place in as little as one lifetime, or else in three, seven or more lifetimes.

The majority of people are incapable of such rapid change and there are few teachers who are able to guide those changes in a student. When a suitable person does meet a competent teacher, and the bond of trust between them is as it should be, the ground for remarkable transformation is present. But in reality such a meeting is quite rare. Should it occur, the teacher, drawing upon the vast range of vajrayana techniques, will devise and monitor a programme of practice which the student must follow to the letter.

This is of vital importance, as the task will not always be an easy one. One needs first to come to know oneself, as one really is and not in the usual way people both underestimate and overestimate themselves. Then one has to face up to and overcome, step by step, one's weaknesses, illusions and blockages. During this process there is no particular need to become a better person artificially, as the dissolution of each negative facet naturally reveals its positive counterpart, just as clouds dissolving reveal the sun. As all goodness is already there within each and every one of us — our buddha nature — there is no need to create it; simply to let it manifest with its own radiance. By removing greed, its natural generosity shines. By taking away the anger that has suppressed it, natural loving kindness is ever present. By taking away self-pity and attachments woven through fear of loneliness, there is natural concern for others and one becomes an impartial friend for all. And so on: the changes are infinite and wonderful, though possibly painful at times. The main qualities required on the part of the disciple are those of faith and diligence. The teacher's qualities are to possess the true teachings of his or her lineage, to have been empowered to teach and therefore to be able to transmit the living power, known as the blessing, of the lineage and to have the compassionate qualities of a bodhisattva.

Throughout this process, vajrayana practice aids one by constantly recalling the presence of the Buddha within. Rather than conceiving of spiritual practice as a *path* which some day will end up where we want to go and which by definition has not yet reached that point, we learn to recognise the immediacy, the *innateness*, of enlightenment in all things. It is like already being where we want to be, but not noticing it because we are lost in a daydream. The task of vajrayana is to awaken us repeatedly from that dream.

At first this immediacy of enlightenment is an intellectual appreciation only. It is through the proper practice of meditation that we approach the truth of inner enlightenment experientially. With time, experiences, which come and go, bring realisation; the mature understanding, fostered by experience, which remains as our basic wisdom. The possibilities of the mind's experience are limitless. It is very easy to mistake many exceptional states for enlightenment and this is why a wise guiding teacher is absolutely indispensable. The story is told of a renowned master in India who was convinced he had achieved mahamudra, the summit of meditation. He meditated within a state of blissful peace for twelve years, only to die and be reborn a cat. He had mistaken a powerful state of personal well-being for enlightenment. It is easy to understand this story, seeing the totally-contented, sensual repleteness of the purring pussy. Only a competent meditation teacher can steer our mental awakening over the years in such a way that true progress is made and so that the mind's true, perfect inner nature can eventually be glimpsed for a first — but vital first — instant, compared by Tilopa to a light that shines in a place which before has only ever known darkness.

Not only that: facing up to enlightenment's truth and to one's mental habits, which constantly mask it like a daydream blotting out reality, requires a courage and a frankness that can only be learnt at the feet of one's teacher, who is like a universal mirror, reflecting uncompromisingly all that one is, Buddha and human combined, with a compassionate patience which keeps him by one's side through trials and tribulations, joys and successes, lifetime after lifetime.

The necessity of having a teacher

It would have been normal to call this section *the necessity of having a guru* but that last word has unfortunately acquired a resonance it ought not to have. Guru is no more than the everyday Indian word for teacher. In small Indian village schools, children address their teachers as *guruji*. Adults learning to play the sitar will call their music masters that too. Although outrages perpetrated from time to time by a few quacks have not spoilt the word doctor, the antics of a few ego-maniacs who have become cult leaders have tainted the word guru: a good word damaged.

Not only do all Buddhist traditions recognise the absolute necessity of having a teacher; it is the obvious resort everywhere in everything. To acquire a skill as quickly as possible, we naturally turn to someone who is already expert in it and who can communicate it well. To try to reinvent or rediscover everything our-selves would be time-wasting and potentially dangerous.

This is particularly true when it comes to working on our own mind; the most precious of all possessions — especially for Buddhists, who believe in reincarna-tion and expect to live many, many lives and therefore to renew their physical bodies over and over again, yet to continue with the same mind. The worst that can happen physically is that we may lose this life and have to start all over again, growing up in another one. Mentally the risk is much greater. We have to live in our mind life after life. Mind is an ongoing continuum that we cannot switch off even for a second. Therefore there is a need for caution and reflection when under-taking anything which may radically affect the mind.

Fragile and capricious, frequently a hotchpotch of contradictions, the human mind is difficult to change; slow to change too. Its transformation needs to be guided in the skilful, loving light shed by another who is already free. As few humans have a mind which is truly liberated, good teachers — good gurus — are rare indeed.

There is much less hierarchy in Tibetan Buddhism than in most religions. Tibetan culture, on the contrary, until the 1950s had an almost medieval hierar-chy in which individuals knew and kept their place. One must be careful not to confuse the two, especially in areas where they overlap. The religion is, for the most part, non-hierarchical in its organisation — there is no one giant pyramidal chain of command and no maternal, all-providing church. This is intimately relat-ed to the style of the Buddhist teachings, in which each person learns to be respon-sible for himself or herself, each monk or nun has to find their own sustenance and each monastery is more or less independent. The type of hierarchy which does exist in Buddhism is one based in respect for accomplishment; recognition in another of erudition or the fruition of meditation.

In this respect, the Karmapa is the guru's guru, endowed with a natural clar-ity and authority which is the refuge of even the greatest teachers. It was a salu-tary experience to witness eminent Buddhist lamas, sometimes renowned for their strictness or powerful presence, become like children with their father when in the presence of the 16th Karmapa. The 17th Karmapa has maintained the same authority. Showing neither fear nor awe before anyone, he refuses any sort of emotional or conventional manipulation. The continuity, in this and other respects, is striking. As Akong Tulku Rinpoche, who spent much time with the 16th Karmapa and who was with the 17th from the time of his recognition onwards for a long period, says:

> In all the times I saw the new Karmapa, either before or after his enthronement as the Karmapa, I cannot find anything which is different from the 16th, whether it be in his way of talking, way of looking or even his way of joking, which is exactly the same as in his previous emanation. He has the same powerful presence, showing absolutely no fear of anyone. When important people or high lamas come, he changes and adapts to the situation, assuming a natural authority, which he has. He will not be dominated by anyone.
>
> I knew the previous Karmapa quite well. Of course, I can only speak about the way he looked at me when he spoke, what he said and how he acted — I cannot pretend to know his mind — but all those things are exactly the same. It is as though he is in a smaller body now and was in a larger body then. That is the only noticeable difference. Even then, the remarkable eyes are the same, each looking different and conveying a different energy. For me, this has been very striking. It does not have to be like this. It can also happen that lamas change from one incarnation to the next but in this case the continuity is undeniable.

◆ ◆ ◆

Gampopa[1] outlines the necessity of having a guru not only by quoting scriptural authority and showing the sheer common sense of it, but also by giving three useful examples. A guru is like a guide in an unknown land, whose presence avoids one's spirituality going off in completely the wrong direction or wasting time in unnecessary detours. A guru is like a bodyguard in a dangerous place, protecting one against loss of valuables or loss of life — the valuables being the goodness one carefully builds up over the years, which can suddenly be destroyed by the likes of anger, confusion or pride, and 'life' in this case being the possibility of a better rebirth next time round. Finally, a guru is like a ferryman, guiding the raft of one's meditation with all the skill of one who knows which treacherous undercurrents to avoid and the favourable winds in which to hoist every sail aboard.

Vajrayana Buddhism is not the sole domain of gurus. In texts of the Theravadin tradition of Buddhism, such as the *Path of Purification*, we read of the necessity of

[1] In *Gems of Dharma, Jewels of Freedom*, Chapter 3

finding a good teacher and of serving that person in humility. This question of humble service can be a difficult pill to swallow in modern times, when cultures are more and more egocentric and humility and humiliation are easily confounded. Paradoxically enough, humility is one the noblest of qualities. If ego is the obstacle to compassion and to enlightenment, how can we not but recourse to humility, pride's antidote, in our quest for liberation? How can we find true humility without the presence of someone and something admirable, because far greater than ourself? Herein lies the key to the guru's presence and that of the lineage he or she represents.

The teacher's role

Buddhas are teachers, not saviours. When one becomes a Buddhist, through the ceremony of *taking refuge*, one takes refuge in the *Buddha* because he is the wisest of teachers. One takes refuge in his teaching, the *dharma*, as the actual way to liberation and in the Buddhist *sangha* as reliable friends willing and able to help one along the path. These three refuges are also known as the three most precious things, or three jewels.

The key idea behind taking refuge in the Buddha is that no one can liberate someone else psychologically. No one can pump in wisdom, liberation, compassion or whatever it may be from the outside, no matter how hard they try. It has to come from within. But what one person *can* do for someone else is to explain how to achieve the wisdom or liberation he himself has achieved. Another person can supply the means but thereafter one has to do the work oneself. The guru's role is to teach the way, just as the Buddha did, in which the student can become what the guru has already become; perhaps even to surpass him.

There is a story of a disciple who assiduously followed the meditation instruction of his lama and who devotedly held his teacher in great esteem. Through his diligent practice in solitude, he eventually mastered the power of the elements and could fly. Winging through space, he returned to his aged teacher and enjoined him to fly with him but then, embarrassed, realised that his teacher had not reached that point yet. By revering his teacher as the Buddha, he had received a Buddha's blessing and reaped all the benefits this brought. In reality, the teacher in his life was the very necessary catalyst for putting him in touch with the Buddha within.

True change only comes about as a result of our own effort. However, the process of change is aided by the fact that we do each have this purity of buddha nature within. It happens sometimes that a little skilful work can open a chink in the fabric of ignorance to let a lot of light shine through. This is the Buddhist explanation of what other religions might consider as divine grace.

To return to the analogy of the three levels of Buddhism given in Chapter 4, using the example of a saucer, teacup and tea: it is obvious that the tea without the teacup and saucer is a mess. A cup is needed to contain the tea. Albeit of fine porcelain which brings out the taste exquisitely, the cup without a saucer burns the hands. A saucer is necessary. Vajrayana Buddhism needs to be practised within the 'container' of the compassionate vision of mahayana. That container needs to be supported by the ethics common to all schools of Buddhism. This means that a vajrayana teacher is a teacher of Buddhism in its entirety. As we saw in Chapter 4, the Karmapa maintains the integrity of the lineages of all three levels of Buddhism through the ages.

The original Tibetan word for guru was lama (*bla.ma*). At the beginning, it seems that this word was reserved solely for the most saintly teachers, those embodying the enlightenment they taught. With the centuries, and through the Tibetan people's own devotion to their teachers, the word has become applied much more broadly, being used as a term of respect for anyone learned or well-experienced in meditation or even simply for a venerable old monk. Keeping within the original definition, a distinction needs to be made between a lama, in the sense of a vajrayana guru, and a 'root-lama', who is one's guiding teacher from here until enlightenment.

These two terms are quite clearly definable. A lama is an accredited holder of a lineage of teachings, who initiates one into that lineage by empowerment (*dbang*), by sacred transmission of scripture (*lung*) and by teachings on the technique of practice (*khrid*). These, especially the first, are the three great tasks of a vajrayana guru and particularly of the Karmapa. Although root lamas may do these things too, they are unique inasmuch as they are the one through whom one first glimpses one's own buddha nature. This usually happens at the end of a long period of training and meditation, all leading up to that revelatory moment when, due to the root-lama, light shines where there had only been darkness before. It is called 'introducing one to the essence of mind' and the lama who does it, having led one to that point, is to play an extraordinary role in one's life. One may have many lamas, but there will only be one root-lama in one's life.

Secret teachings

The methods of vajrayana are potent. Like anything powerful, they are dangerous. This fact, appreciated sanely, needs to be savoured. Electricity can be lethal, yet we have learnt to surround ourselves with it, wall-sockets in every room, and to enjoy in security its manifold powers. Driving a car can be dangerous yet hundreds of vehicles can whizz along in close proximity to each other, providing the drivers learn the right codes of behaviour. Aeroplanes can take us far away with astonishing rapidity, yet we must respect the fact that, even if our legs ache, it is unwise to open the door to go for a stroll outside during the flight!

Working intensively upon one's mind under the guidance of an experienced and competent teacher is potentially the most rewarding of all human endeavours. We need to learn how not to short-circuit the processes set in motion, just as children need to learn not to put their fingers in the wall-sockets. We need to learn the right codes of conduct, so that we glide smoothly along the highway, alongside others doing the same. We need to know how not to give up in mid-journey, when the risks to our sanity could be inestimable.

Vajrayana teachings are secret. In fact they are called *self-secret*. This is for several reasons. The main one lies in the nature of the teachings themselves. When the time is right for an individual, his or her mind can open to new understanding. Before then, no matter what is said or done, the penny does not — cannot — drop. Because each stage and aspect of awakening only makes real sense to the mind mature enough to grasp it, it is self-secret to any mind not yet at that point. Therefore, no matter how many books are written revealing the innermost 'secrets' or techniques of vajrayana, they can never make experiential sense to a mind that is not ready. Only a poor intellectual replica is created, like a child's plastic toy which the infant can pretend is the real thing but which, in reality, is useless.

Vajrayana teachings and practices are also secret because they are customised for each individual. Outside the intimate relationship which exists between teacher and disciple, they have no sense. Just as a doctor's prescription and advice on diet and behaviour is tailor-made to the patient, so also is a programme of meditation, guidance in personal conduct and so forth purpose-built for the disciple. Just as it is pointless for one patient to take the pills of another after observing that the other person seems to be getting better on them, so is it pointless trying to compare one's own personal story and transformation with that of someone else.

We are each unique and, to boot, that uniqueness changes all the time. What happens in another person's mind is impenetrable. At best, only a very wise guru will understand what is happening, as well as all the past background and future potential in which that 'happening' takes place. His advice, and the techniques, empowerments and so forth which are the channels of that advice, are by their very nature secret. The words 'confidence' and 'confidential' hold a tremendous significance here.

The Karmapa has an influence so vast that it would be impossible for him to be the personal mentor of many ordinary individuals. The spiritual meeting that most people have with him takes place either through receiving empowerment (*dbang*), participating in the Vajra Crown ceremony (see Chapter 15), receiving refuge or bodhisattva vow or through what are known as 'the four liberating actions': seeing, hearing, touching and thinking of him. These latter can take place simultaneously during a 'blessing', when people prostrate, offer traditional white silk scarves and receive his hand upon their head as a blessing. However, many lamas will encourage their disciples to think of the Karmapa as their root-lama, when they are doing visualisation meditation that includes an image of one's root lama and therefore many Kagyu followers feel tremendously close to the Karmapa, as the blessing they experience when setting the mind on him is undeniable and pure.

Empowerment

There is much that could be said about empowerment, but most of it is self-secret and, like so many self-secret and profound things, it is better to say nothing and to leave the mind in a state of pristine receptivity for when the right time comes. Too many words and explanations clutter the mind with unnecessary preconceptions. They in their turn lead to expectation and anxiety, which will confuse one's appreciation of the 'real thing' when it comes along.

What is often explained publicly about empowerment is that it fulfils two functions: it opens the door to a specific practice and it conveys a blessing. For those dedicated to vajrayana Buddhist practice, it is very necessary to receive an empowerment before undertaking any of its sadhana methods intensively. The empowerment conveys the protection and blessing of the lineage, without which the practice can never succeed. In Milarepa's life story we read how, at one point, he tries to take a short cut in his development and goes to a lama other than his own guru, Marpa the Translator, with a forged letter asking him to pass on the instructions for a certain practice. Although he performed every aspect of the technique diligently, the normal signs of achievement did not manifest and eventually his new teacher guessed what had happened.

In vajrayana Buddhism, there are three extra refuges; three special instances of the ordinary refuges. The *guru*, the Buddha's presence in one's life, is the source of 'blessing'. The *yidams*, the special facet of dharma, are the source of specific accomplishments. The *protectors*, the special sangha, are the source of skilful activity. These three refuges are called the *three sources* or the *three roots*.

A guru is described as the source of all blessing. In this context, blessing has nothing of its usual vague feeling of something spiritually uplifting. It is the transmission of realisation. All realisation comes through the guru's kindness and patience, but more particularly through the power of lineage which he embodies. Without the connection to the source that the lineage blessing provides, practice is virtually fruitless, as Milarepa discovered the hard way. The lineage blessing is transmitted through empowerment and afterwards, once one has received the scriptural transmission and instructions, one is fully entitled to practise. This is the first role of empowerment and it corresponds, more or less, to the notion of initiation. 'Empowerment' can sound too grand and one might well expect to feel some transmission of power immediately and thus be disappointed. It is merely the sowing of a seed, which only the water of diligent practice will help grow into a beautiful tree.

The second purpose of empowerment is similar, but more remote. It makes a

HH the 17th Karmapa giving the 'standing Chenresig' empowerment

connection and conveys a blessing in the more ordinary sense of the word. It still sows a seed but that seed may not encounter the right water and sunshine until some time way in the future. An empowerment in this sense carries no or little commitment with it, whereas the first sort usually requires some sort of practice commitment from the person who has requested empowerment.

There is a much deeper sense of empowerment, in which something truly powerful does happen between guru and disciple and they share in an experience of the true meaning of whatever it is the empowerment concerns. It is right to mention this but little more can be conveyed in print.

The methods of vajrayana

The best way for the reader to get the feel of vajrayana method is to read the life-stories of the early masters of the Kagyu lineage; that is why they exist. Having read their stories, one thing stands out — it was different for each of them. That is perhaps the greatest teaching. Whatever rubbish is still clogging up one's mind has to be removed, one way or another. The guru's task is to help the disciple to remove it as skilfully and quickly as possible, using whatever means are appropriate. These can be traditional techniques of sadhana, involving visualisation, mantra recitation and so forth. They can be the practices of physical yogas and breathing techniques. They can be meditations focused directly on the mechanics of mind itself. They can also be hilarious or dramatic circumstances in which the guru helps the disciple see himself or herself in very unexpected ways.

The reader is heartily commended to read the biographies of Tilopa, Naropa, Marpa, Milarepa and Gampopa. They are stories which live joyfully in the heart,

and teach from within through all of one's life. The reader is also warned to beware of advice, from other people or in books, which says, *first you do this, then that, then a three-year retreat . . .* as though there was a single conveyor belt in a religious factory along which we all pass to be processed.

Vajrayana practice mobilises the whole of one's body, speech and mind, setting them to good use. The body sits in meditation posture or does prostrations and these are excellent for bringing its constitutive elements into harmony and purifying physical errors of the past. Speech is used in meaningful prayer or mantra, which is the very quintessence of prayer, and this is powerful in purifying the subconscious traces left by past misuse of that magnificent capacity we have as humans, to communicate and speak. The mind is fully mobilised — not just the intellect but everything the mind does, and in particular its ability to imagine and to interpret the messages brought in by the senses. This is where visualisation comes into play. Besides the transformation of the ordinary activities of mind, there is the opening up of areas previously unknown: the experience of lasting peace, stability of crystal clear perception and analysis within that peace, and a gradual penetration into the endless subtleties of meditation that will lead to wisdom.

The possibilities of vajrayana practice are limitless; there are so many hundreds of techniques. A competent teacher is the only person able to know which to apply, when, and for how long.

Chapter Eleven

The Early Patriarchs in India and Tibet

"One instant with the guru is worth aeons of perfection-stage meditation"

Naropa

Naropa's life is very reminiscent of the twelve stages of the life of the Buddha. A bodhisattva of the highest, i.e. tenth, level, the future Naropa realised that the time had come to enter the human life that would bring him to full enlightenment. In the clarity of his meditation, he could see his future father, the Buddhist king Santivarman, who longed for a son and who himself bore some physical signs of an enlightened being. His future mother dreamt of voidness and bliss inseparable and  of light filling the entire country. Some time later, Naropa was born, his body bearing the marks of a future Buddha. The earth shook, many rainbows appeared and thunder rumbled. It was approximately the year 1016, in Bengal.

At the age of eight, disgusted by worldliness, he went to study dharma in Kashmir. By 11, he had become a brilliant scholar. Returning to his country, the erudite prince taught Buddhist ethics to his people. His desire-free mind was devoted to Buddhism and quite content. However, at the age of 17 he was virtually forced into marriage by his parents, who were anxious for an heir. His wife became his disciple and at the age of 25 he definitively renounced the world and became a novice monk and, at 31, a bhikkhu. The former royal child prodigy studied at Pullahari monastery and eventually his renown led to his becoming abbot of the great Nalanda monastery. His personal radiance inspired many people to set foot on the path. He was the ideal abbot.

However, after some eight years he had a vision of a leprous old hag 'with 37 ugly features' who informed him that she was saddened because he understood the teachings only intellectually, not in reality. He realised that he was seeing the reflection of his own 37 worldly impurities, and declared:

"Samsara is to see fault in others."

He knew it was time to leave all and set out to find his guru, to complete his enlightenment. Despite everyone's impassioned entreaties he left Nalanda at the age of 42. There followed a long series of trials, in which he constantly met strange phenomena symbolic of his own remaining blockages due to preconceived ideas about ultimate reality. These were often vivid and painful learning processes, representing the untying of karmic knots. In each of these episodes he glimpsed brief visions of his guru, pointing out his mistakes. In fact, in one form or another, his guru Tilopa had been with him ever since he had seen the old leper woman, and at the end of these first trials, they met properly. The first real teaching that Naropa received from Tilopa consisted of the latter saying nothing but, in a powerful dialogue of minds, showing twelve symbolic acts, each of which Naropa interpreted correctly. Then Tilopa gave him empowerments and personal teachings, including one special instruction, preparing the ground for what was to follow:

> *"Don't look for bliss, or its opposite."*

Then followed the twelve main teachings. Each of these shows a profound contact between Naropa and Tilopa, which means, in reality, between Naropa and the purity of his own mind. Each starts with a painful trial, instigated by Tilopa, which reveals a defect in Naropa and for which a teaching is given and then practised for about a year. For instance, in the first trial, Tilopa instructs Naropa to climb up onto a temple roof and jump off it. Faithful Naropa does just this. His guru then heals his shattered body with his blessing and gives him the teachings known as the 'Wish-fulfilling Gem'. The twelve teachings, most of which have since become the core of the inner Kagyu transmission, were:

1. The 'wish-fulfilling gem': a very complete form of purification
2. 'Same-taste', showing the presence of the enlightened essence within all and everything
3. Commitment: maintaining a pure relationship (*samaya*) with one's guru, everything and everyone
4. *Tummo:* purification of the subtle inner body of chakra and nadi
5. Illusory body yoga: bringing wisdom into one's perception of reality
6. Dream yoga: how to understand and master dreams, using them to purify karma and develop enlightened action
7. Radiant light yoga
8. Transference of consciousness, particularly at the time of death (*po.wa*)
9. Resurrection
10. Great bliss yoga: control of sexual energy and realisation of the common essence of samsara and nirvana, of pain and happiness. It is on mastering this teaching that he received the name Naropa.
11. Mahamudra and
12.. 'Transitory Phase' yoga (*bar.do*): teaching on how to be enlightened in every phase of existence — life, death, after-death, etc.

Through mastering these twelve Naropa's mind became almost totally identified with the enlightened mind of his guru Tilopa, who then sent him away to meditate further and help all beings. Naropa did this for some time, performing many miracles, and eventually returned to Tilopa, who removed the last remaining traces of impurity in Naropa's mind — in particular the latter's feeling of a need to meditate — by revealing to him, in all its fullness, mind's innate purity since beginningless time. Naropa then declared:

"One need ask no more when actuality is seen."

Fully enlightened, he became known as a 'second Buddha' and wrought great benefit for many beings. In particular, Tilopa instructed him to bring Marpa, the Tibetan, to enlightenment. Through Naropa and Marpa, the *father tantra*, the *guhyasamaja*, was taken to Tibet, as well as exceedingly pure transmissions of other tantras, such as that of *Chakrasamvara*.

Naropa passed away, literally, at Pullahari, his enlightened body fading back into voidness amid myriad rainbows and beautiful celestial music. His life was an intense example of the power of faith — essential to the swiftest path of mahamudra within Kagyu Buddhism. By perfectly following his guru's advice and maintaining his dedicated commitment, he completed his journey to enlightenment.

Marpa

Marpa, born in 1012 in south central Tibet, was the first Tibetan patriarch of the Kagyu tradition — which is often called the *Marpa Kagyu* in his honour. He was also the first Patriarch who would reappear again and again in the lineage. Marpa is believed to have been the mahasiddhas Dombipa, Sri Simha and Darikapa in previous lives in India. In 8th-century Tibet he was the astrologer who chose the site of Samye monastery. Later he was reborn as Dharma Semang, one of Guru Rinpoche's secretaries,  writer of *terma* and expert in wrathful practices. Then he became Marpa, during the 11th-century restoration of dharma, and subsequently other masters, including the famous Taranatha. In the Kagyu tradition, besides being Marpa he was also to become:

— Drogon Rechen, to whom the first Karmapa handed his prediction letter,
— Yeshe Ö, the second Karmapa's disciple who found the hidden land of Sari,
— The golden lineage holder Ratnabhadra, guru of the fourth Karmapa, and
— Choji Gyaltsen, who was given the title 'Tai Situ' by the Chinese Emperor Yung Lo (Ch'eng Tsu) in the early 15th century. The incarnations have been known as Tai Situpa ever since.

Marpa's determination was strong, even as a child. In order to acquire Buddhist teachings for his country, he made three journeys to India. This was no mean feat at the time, as the dangers and health risks of travel were great. To acquire for Tibet the good karma that would assure that those teachings would take root there, he put a lot of energy into collecting offerings from its people to take to Indian masters. In order to accomplish properly his task of acquiring and translating teachings, he spent three years in Nepal, acclimatising to humidity and heat as well as the lower altitude. During his stay he learnt more than thirty Indian dialects.

His main teacher in India was Naropa. He spent 16 years and 7 months studying under his guidance, during which time he received the full transmission of all that Naropa had received from Tilopa. Furthermore, Naropa sent him to other gurus, especially Maitripa, Jnanagarbha, Kukuripa, and the wisdom dakini of Sosarling. He received each of their special dharma transmissions: the complete mind teachings of mahamudra, Guhyasamaja, Mahamaya and Dorje Denshi. Although he could have received all of those lineages from Naropa himself, Naropa wanted him to go to the best specialists of the day in each practice, so that the teachings Marpa carried to Tibet would be charged to the greatest extent possible with lineage blessing.

From Naropa himself he received the Hevajra tantra and Naropa's special techniques — the essence of vajrayana taught him by Tilopa and above all the full transmission of the Chakrasamvara tantra. Marpa not only learnt but practised and gained results in these and many other vajrayana teachings. In particular, Naropa helped Marpa to break through the conceptual blockages preventing his complete liberation and thereby brought him to total enlightenment. In their oneness of enlightenment, he shared the vast treasury of his mind with Marpa.

Naropa made Marpa his dharma regent for Tibet and entrusted him with the task of bringing a very exceptional being, Milarepa, to enlightenment. It is said that Naropa himself prostrated towards Tibet when Marpa told him of his disciple Milarepa.

Marpa had always hoped that his own son, Dharma Doday, would become his spiritual heir but Naropa informed him that this was not to be. The Kagyu tradition is not a spiritual succession based upon family dynasties, as other lineages in Tibet were in the past and, in part, still are. In fact, one of the reasons why the second Karmapa was given prominence by the Chinese Emperor was because the Karmapa was self-recognised and could be born into any family. The Chinese empire of the time was tired of sending endless gifts to religious dynastic families, which were too powerful for their liking.

After his three journeys and 21 years in India, Marpa spent the last years of his life firmly establishing in Tibet the teachings he had secured. He had four highly gifted disciples, each specialised in different domains. His main heir, who received everything from him, just as he himself had from Naropa, was Jetsun Milarepa.

Milarepa

Milarepa's moving and inspiring life story is the most acces-
sible of all the Tibetan biographies published to date. It
stands as a gripping story in its own right and it is highly
commended to the reader. Milarepa was born in 1052 into
comfortable circumstances but, while still a child, saw the
life of his immediate family shattered by the death of his
father and subsequent takeover of the family assets by an
avaricious uncle and aunt, who thereafter used Milarepa,
his sister and his mother as slaves. Milarepa's mother
patiently awaited his coming of age to reclaim the family land, house and wealth,
but when the time came this proved unsuccessful. The only way she could imagine the injustice being righted was for her son to learn magic and curse the relatives. She threatened suicide if Milarepa did not do as she asked.

Milarepa went away and fulfilled his mother's wishes. Magical demons conjured up by him destroyed his uncle's house during a feast, killing 25 members
of his family. Milarepa let it be known that the nightmarish wrecking of their
home was his work and threatened to do worse if his family's house and land
were not restored. Despite the fear he had inspired, it was dangerous for Milarepa
to remain in the area and so he returned to his teacher.

The latter was ageing and starting to regret the darker deeds that he and his
disciples had wrought. He placed his hope in Milarepa, feeling that this determined and good-hearted young man might achieve the salvation of both of them.
He sent him to dharma teachers to learn virtue and, above all, purification of mis-
deeds. This eventually led Milarepa to meet Marpa.

·Marpa gave the repentant mass murderer a rough time, insisting that he build
a tower for him. As soon as it was built, he made him tear it down. This was
repeated several times, with towers of different shapes. In the end Marpa insisted on a great castle tower, eight stories high, before he would give Milarepa any
formal teachings. This seemingly cruel exploitation was, in fact, his way of helping Milarepa purify the bad karma. Using one or two simple tools and his bare
hands, Milarepa slaved until he was all but broken, physically and morally. At
one point he even ran away in desperation, but he never lost faith. In the end,
after the hardest of all spiritual apprenticeships and with the tower almost completed, he was admitted among Marpa's students. He was given ordination and
teachings and entered solitary retreat, where he meditated with a butter-lamp on
his head, not being allowed to move until the lamp burnt out. He gained good
results and Marpa eventually sent him to meditate in isolated caves and mountain fastnesses for many years.

Milarepa's diligence and faith were second to none. Through them he achieved
something exceedingly rare, in fact almost unique: he attained enlightenment in
a single lifetime. Famous for his mastery of Naropa's *six yogas*, he performed

many miracles such as flying through space, passing through rocks and living for months in the snows at some 5,000 metres sustained only by life-breath while wearing nothing but a thin cotton cloth, hence his name: Mila was his family name and *repa* means *one clad in cotton*. An itinerant hermit, he was the perfect example of the Buddhist mendicant yogi. His enlightened songs, one of the greatest treasuries of Kagyu teaching, have been an inspiration for many people since their publication in English. He had one disciple (Gampopa) like the sun, one (Rechungpa) like the moon, 25 like stars and many thousands of others.

Gampopa

We have seen something of Gampopa in the *samadhiraja-sutra* chapter. This tenth-level bodhisattva was born in central Tibet in 1079 as the son of a very wise doctor. As a teenager he completed his own medical training and gained proficiency in several meditation practices of the Nyingma tradition. In his early twenties he married and fathered a son and a daughter. However, his wife and both children died after catching an incurable disease that was sweeping the area. His wife made him promise to become a monk after her death and this he did.

He became the monk *Precious Virtue* and spent an intensive period of time travelling and studying under excellent teachers of mahayana Buddhist philosophy and vajrayana technique. In particular, he benefited from the Khadampa teachings brought to Tibet by Atisa Dipankara. He could meditate comfortably for many days without moving or needing food or drink and his presence was one of great peace and finesse. However, he then started to have visions of a ragged yogi; visions which uplifted him to states he had never before experienced. The increasing intensity of these episodes caused him to leave everything behind and set off in search of the yogi, whom by now he knew to be Milarepa. In a strange world where meditation experience intermingled indistinguishably with his perception of reality, he made his way through a series of highly-meaningful symbolic experiences until he eventually encountered his guru.

Milarepa had inner knowledge that Gampopa would be his future spiritual heir long before the latter's arrival and realised what a magnificent and virtuous being he was. Over the next years, in a relatively short period of time, Milarepa passed on all his teachings to him and supervised his progress with great love and care. He even gave him the ultimate initiation, into diligence, by showing him the hard skin and callouses on his bottom where he had sat meditating for months and years on end on wild, rocky mountainsides until attaining realisation. When he had taught Precious Virtue all he could, he sent him to Mount Gampo, with instruction on how to meditate there. He told him the signs of achievement by which he would know that it was time to teach others and predicted that a great number of people would eventually gather there as his disciples.

The man of Mt Gampo — Gampopa — achieved his enlightenment there and soon many people came to seek his advice. He established the very first Tibetan Kagyu monastery in that place and taught dharma on all its levels, from the very basics through to vajrayana. By bringing the monastic training and the erudition of the Khadampas into the Kagyu transmission, he had fortified and broadened it, fulfilling in part Naropa's prophecy that it would go from strength to strength in its next generations. Gampopa had many eminent scholars and yogis among his disciples. The most renowned was His Holiness the First Karmapa, Dusum Chenpa.

Chapter Twelve

The First Fifteen Karmapas

The Karmapas are revered as being the manifestation of all the Buddhas' enlightened activity. Their presence in the world over the past eight centuries has been the most perfect example of three points quintessential to Buddhism, known generally as *basis*, *path* and *fruition*. The teachings on *basis* explain the good news that all beings have the essence of enlightenment within them, and the bad news that it is, for the most part, hidden away and unrecognised. How the various emotional and conceptual blockages hiding it can be removed is explained through the teachings on the *path* of Buddhist practice. *Fruition* describes the fully-exposed enlightened essence shining in all its qualities.

The notions of basis, path and fruition, which can be applied to all traditions of Buddhism, are extremely important in vajrayana. Although all Buddhas are the same in essence, when appearing as Karmapas they are particularly skilled in vividly demonstrating those three principles, by awakening beings to their inner potential, by teaching the profoundest of paths and by demonstrating their own qualities of fruition with great confidence. The following is but a brief glimpse of the lives of the first fifteen Karmapas. The fuller accounts in Lama Karma Thinley's excellent book *The History of the Sixteen Karmapas of Tibet* are heartily commended to the reader and I am indebted to Khenchen Thrangu Rinpoche for his explanations, upon which the following is based.

The 1st Gyalwa Karmapa, Dusum Chenpa (1110-1193) was a gifted child who studied and practised dharma intently from an early age. Already quite learned by the age of twenty, he became a monk and studied the sutras and tantra intensively for a further ten years. At thirty, he went to Daklha Gampo — Gampopa's monastery — to receive teachings from him. Although this was an historic meeting of two great Buddhist bodhisattvas emanating on Earth with a profound purpose, Gampopa nevertheless first made Dusum Chenpa train in the foundation practices of the Khadampa tradition and, following that, in the general philosophy of the sutras. This set a fine example for all future Kagyu followers and showed the need for the correct basis of knowledge even when — especially when — one does the most powerful of vajrayana practices.

The first Karmapa received empowerments and instruction in the Hevajra tantra and spent four years in strict retreat, training in the peaceful stability (*samatha*) and profound insight (*vipasyana*) aspects of meditation. He then received the full transmission of the inner instructions of the Kagyu tradition. In nine days he absorbed what Naropa had received over 12 years from Tilopa. Rechungpa, the 'moon-like' disciple of Milarepa, also instructed him, principally in the Six

Yogas of Naropa. His attainment in one of these — *tummo,* inner-heat — was particularly boosted by his own natural compassion and produced rapid results. Following his teacher's instruction he then went away to meditate.

Gampopa eventually died and Dusum Chenpa returned to Daklha Gampo to honour his remains. He had a powerful vision of his teacher and knew that it was time to implement one of his final instructions: to go to the place where he would achieve enlightenment — Kampo Kangra — and there to practise mahamudra. He promised that he would live until the age of 84, in order to benefit the dharma. He achieved enlightenment at the age of fifty, while practising dream yoga. He had a vision at that time of the celestial beings (*dakini*) offering him a vajra crown woven from their hair. His name — Dusum Chenpa — means *Knower of the Past, Present and Future,* referring to the total lucidity he attained at enlightenment, giving him knowledge of the three modes of time, and the 'timeless time' of enlightened awareness.

From then onwards his teaching activity was intense. At the age of 58 he founded a monastery at Kampo Nénang. He later established an important seat at Karma Gön in eastern Tibet and, at the age of 74, another seat at Tsurphu in central Tibet, in the valley of the Tolung, which feeds into the Brahmaputra. It is interesting to note, in the light of the 16th Karmapa's prediction letter, that the abbot of the Buddhist monastery at Bodh Gaya, in India, the place of the Buddha's enlightenment, sent a conch shell to Dusum Chenpa at Tsurphu, as a token of the latter's significance for buddhadharma. This conch shell symbolism is found in many stories of the 16 Karmapas.

The 1st Karmapa, Dusum Chenpa, made predictions about future Karmapas. In particular, he was the first Karmapa to present a prediction letter detailing his future incarnation. He gave it to his main disciple, Drogon Rechen, predecessor of the Tai Situ line (they were only called Tai Situ after this title was conferred by the Chinese emperor in the early 15th century). He passed away at the age of 84, as predicted. His heart was found intact in the funeral pyre and some of his remaining bones bore self-manifesting shapes of Buddhas. (The similarities with the passing of the 16th Karmapa are remarkable.) Among his other main disciples were Tak-lungpa, founder of the Ta-lung Kagyu, Tsangpa Gyare, founder of the Drukpa Kagyu (widespread in Bhutan these days) and Lama Khadampa Deshek, founder of the Katok Nyingma lineage.

The 2nd Gyalwa Karmapa, Karma Pakshi (1206-1283) was a child prodigy who had already acquired a broad understanding of dharma philosophy and meditation by the age of ten. His teacher, Pomdrakpa, had received the full Kagyu transmission from Drogon Rechen, the first Karmapa's spiritual heir. Pomdrakpa realised, through certain very clear visions, that the child in his charge was the reincarnation of Dusum Chenpa, as indicated in the letter given to Drogon Rechen. The young Karma Pakshi assimilated the deepest teachings effortlessly and required only one reading of a text to be familiar with it. He was already enlightened. Nevertheless, Pomdrakpa made a point of formally passing on all the teachings through the traditional empowerments, so that the stream of empowerment lineage would be unbroken. This has been the case ever since: despite their innate clarity, young Karmapas receive all the transmissions formally. The second Karmapa spent much of the first half of his life in meditation retreat. He also visited and restored the monasteries established by the first Karmapa and is famous for having introduced to the Tibetan people communal chanting of the OM MANI PADME HUNG mantra of compassion.

At the age of 47 he set out on a three-year journey to China, in response to an invitation from Kublai, grandson of Ghengis Khan. While there, he performed many spectacular miracles and played an important role as a peacemaker. Although requested to reside there permanently, he declined, not wishing to be the cause of sectarian conflicts with the Sakyapas, whose influence was strong in China at that time. Over the next ten years the Karmapa travelled widely in China, Mongolia and Tibet and became famous as a teacher. He was particularly honoured by Munga Khan, Kublai's brother, who ruled at that time and whom the Karmapa recognised as a former disciple. After Munga's death, Kublai became the Khan. He established the city of Cambalu, the site of present-day Beijing, from which he ruled a vast empire stretching as far as Burma, Korea and Tibet. However, he bore a grudge against the Karmapa, who had refused his invitation to remain in China some years before and had been so close to his brother. He ordered his arrest.

Each attempt to capture, or even kill, the Karmapa was thwarted by the latter's miracles. At one point the Karmapa 'froze' a battalion of 37,000 soldiers on the spot, by using the power of mudra, yet all the time showing compassion. He eventually let himself be captured and put in exile, knowing that his miracles and compassion would eventually lead to Kublai Khan having a change of heart — which did in fact happen. Returning to Tibet towards the end of his life, he had an enormous (16-metre) statue of the Buddha built at Tsurphu, to fulfil a dream he had had long before. The finished work was slightly tilted and Karma Pakshi straightened it by sitting first in the same tilted posture as the statue and then righting himself. The statue moved as he moved. Before dying, he told his main disciple, Urgyenpa, details concerning the next Karmapa's birth.

The 3rd Gyalwa Karmapa, Rangjung Dorje (1284-1339) produced a black crown from nowhere at the age of three and announced that he was the Karmapa, telling his young friends that they were indulging in worldliness. At five, he went to see Urgyenpa, who had dreamt of him the night before and was prepared for his visit. He grew up in Tsurphu receiving not only the full Kagyu transmission but also that of the Nyingma tradition. Having spent some time on the slopes of Mount Everest in retreat and then taken full ordination, he further broadened his studies at a great seat of Khadampa learning.

Rangjung Dorje had a tremendous thirst for learning from the greatest scholars and experts of his day. His approach embraced all traditions of knowledge
and he had an intelligence and sensitivity which could assimilate and compare
all that he studied. Through visions he received of the 'Wheel of Time' (*Kalacakra*)
teachings, he introduced a revised system of astrology. He studied and mastered
medicine. In particular, his mastery of the profound Nyingmapa teachings of
Vimalamitra meant that, in him, the Kagyu *mahamudra* and the Nyingma equivalent, *dzog.chen*, became as one. By the end of his studies, he had learnt and mastered nearly all of the Buddhist teachings brought to Tibet from India by all the
various masters of both the ancient and restoration periods. In the light of that
eclectic wisdom, he composed many significant texts, the most famous of which
is perhaps the Profound Inner Meaning (*zab.mo.nang.don*), pin-pointing the very
essence of vajrayana.

He visited China and there enthroned his disciple, the new emperor Toghon
Temur. Through long-life elixir received from the Karmapa, who returned to
Samye especially to procure it, the emperor was the longest-lived of all the Mongol emperors of China. Rangjung Dorje established many monasteries in Tibet
and China. He died in China and is famous for having appeared in the moon on
the night of his passing.

The 4th Gyalwa Karmapa, Rolpi Dorje (1340-1383) While pregnant, the 4th
Karmapa's mother could hear the sound of the mantra OM MANI PADME HUNG
coming from her womb. The baby said the mantra as soon as it was born. His
early life was full of miracles and manifested a total continuity of the teachings
and qualities of his former incarnation. He could read books and received many
profound teachings in his dreams. While in his teens he received the formal transmissions of both the Kagyu and Nyingma lineages from the great Nyingma guru
Yungtönpa, the third Karmapa's spiritual heir, now very advanced in years. At
the age of 19, he accepted Toghon Temur's passionate invitation to return to China.
After a long and impressive journey, with many halts to give teachings, he arrived
at the imperial palace. He gave teachings in China for three years and established
many temples and monasteries there.

On his return to Tibet, while in the Tsongkha region, Rolpi Dorje gave lay ordination to a very special child whom he predicted to be of great importance to
Buddhism in Tibet. This was Kunga Nyingpo — 'Tsong Khapa' — future founder
of the Gelugpa school, famous for its Dalai Lamas. When Temur died, the Mongol dynasty ended and the Ming dynasty began. The new emperor invited Rolpi
Dorje, who declined the invitation but sent a holy lama in his stead. Rolpi Dorje
composed wonderful mystic songs throughout his life and was an accomplished
poet, fond of Indian poetics. He is also remembered for creating a huge painting
(*thangka*) following a vision of one of his students, who had imagined a Buddha

image over a hundred metres tall. The Karmapa, on horseback, traced the Buddha's outline with hoofprints. The design was measured and traced on cloth. It took 500 workers more than a year to complete the thangka, which depicted the Buddha, Maitreya and Manjusri: the founders of mahayana.

The 5th Gyalwa Karmapa, Deshin Shekpa (1384-1415) was also heard reciting mantras and the Sanskrit alphabet whilst in his mother's womb. He was the wonder child of yogin parents. He received the full transmissions of his lineage and soon completed his traditional training. At the age of 22, he received a moving invitation from Emperor Yung Lo (also known as Ch'eng-Tsu), who had had a vision of him as Avalokitesvara. It took three years for him to reach the imperial palace, where he was warmly received by ten thousand monks. The combination of Yung Lo's devotion and the Karmapa's spirituality produced some extraordinary events: a hundred days of miracles that on the order of the emperor were recorded for posterity as silk paintings with a commentary in five languages. Following this, Deshin Shekpa made a pilgrimage to the famous Wu-tai Shan holy mountains, as the previous two Karmapas had done, to visit his monasteries there.

The 5th Karmapa saved Tibet from bloody war on several occasions by dissuading the emperor from imposing a single religious system there and by pointing out the value of alternative systems, suited to different mentalities. The emperor himself soon became an accomplished bodhisattva and one day, in purity of vision, saw the celestial vajra crown above his guru's head. So that all beings might benefit from seeing something of this transcendent aspect of the Karmapa, he had a physical replica of it made, presented it to his guru and requested him to wear it on special occasions to bring liberation to those who saw it. This was the origin of the Vajra Crown ceremony.

In 1408 Deshin Shekpa set out for Tibet. There he supervised the reconstruction of Tsurphu, damaged by an earthquake, and stimulated the buddhadharma. He spent three years in contemplative retreat. Realising that he would die at a young age, he left indications of his future rebirth and died at 31. The bones left in the ashes of his funeral pyre bore naturally-formed images of many Buddhas.

The 6th Gyalwa Karmapa, Tongwa Donden (1416-1453) The miraculous birth, prodigious qualities and formal education of the 6th Karmapa echoed those of his predecessors. As a young man, he integrated the Shangpa Kagyu and the Shijay (the renowned practice of *gcod* — 'cutting through egotism') lineages into the Kagyu mainstream. He was a visionary who had many significant insights into Avalokitesvara, Tara and other aspects of enlightenment. He composed many prayers for use in the traditional practices of his own lineage and thereby established a body of Kamtsang liturgy. Tongwa Donden's life was mainly dedicated to this literary work and to travelling within Tibet, founding and restoring monasteries, having sacred books printed and strengthening the sangha. Realising that he would die at an early age, he entered retreat, making Gyaltsab Rinpoche his regent and giving him indications of where he would next take birth. His main spiritual heir was Bengar Jampal Zangpo, composer of the famous 'Short Prayer to Vajradhara', frequently used in modern Kagyu centres. The prayer represents his spontaneous utterance upon realising mahamudra and homes in on the very heart of the practice.

The 7th Gyalwa Karmapa, Cheudrak Gyamtso (1454-1506) was heard to say *A ma la* (mother) when born and to declare *AH HUNG, there is nothing in the world but voidness* at five months of age. At nine months his parents took him to Gyaltsab Rinpoche, who recognised the new Karmapa incarnation. When only some five years of age, he brought peace to the southernmost parts of the Tibetan plateau, where the people of Nagaland and Bhutan were at war. He worked hard for the protection of animals and instigated all sorts of projects, such as the construction of bridges. In particular, he encouraged individuals and groups of people to recite many millions of Mani mantras — "The best cure for anything."

Chodrak Gyamtso spent much of his life in retreat or half-retreat. He was an extremely erudite scholar and author and it was he who founded the monastic university at Tsurphu. He also restored the large statue commissioned by Karma Pakshi. Often a peacemaker, he is remembered for his visions of Guru Rinpoche which led him to discover hidden valleys of refuge for people in times of war. He maintained contact with the remaining Buddhists of India and sent much gold to Bodh Gaya for the Buddha image there to be gilded. Knowing that he would pass away at the age of 52, he left details of his next incarnation and passed on the lineage to Tai Situ Tashi Paljor.

The 8th Gyalwa Karmapa, Michö Dorje (1507-1554) was heard to say *Karmapa* at birth. This was reported to the Tai Situpa who confirmed the child to be the new Karmapa but asked the parents to keep this fact secret for three months, to protect the young incarnation. He devised a test, which the baby not only passed but to which he was heard to say *E ma ho! Have no doubts, I am the Karmapa.* He spent the next years at Karma Gön. When he was five, another postulant for the Karmapa title was put forward in Amdo. The Karmapa's regent, Gyaltsab Rinpoche, set out from Tsurphu to investigate the two children. However, on meeting Michö Dorje, he found himself spontaneously prostrating and knew that he was the real Karmapa. He enthroned him the following year.

The 8th Karmapa had many visions during his life revealing the inseparability of his own emanations and those of Guru Rinpoche, both being the emanations of Buddhas to accomplish enlightened activity for however long their teachings are extant. Thus he saw he had been the Guru Rinpoche of the former Buddha Dipamkara and, in general, the activity-aspect of all thousand Buddhas of our universe.

Michö Dorje was one of the most renowned of the Karmapas, being a powerful meditation master, a prolific and erudite scholar, and author of some thirty important works, including very significant texts on the profoundest philosophy known to Buddhism: the *devoid of other* (*gzhan.stong*) view. This represents the zenith of the Middle Way (madhyamika) school of mahayana Buddhism and is a valuable antidote for misunderstandings of voidness. He expounded this view at length and debated it with scholars of other Buddhist tendencies. Michö Dorje was also a visionary artist, to whom we owe the Karma Gadri style of thangka painting — a very spacious, transparent and meditative style. He also composed one of the main devotional practices of the Kagyu school, known as the Four-Session Guru Yoga.

He had been invited to China when quite young, but declined, knowing that the emperor would be dead by the time of his arrival. His refusal offended the envoys carrying the invitation, who returned to China only to find that his prescience was correct. The emperor had died.

Realising the imminence of his own passing, he entrusted a letter of prediction to the Shamarpa and passed away at the age of 47.

The 9th Gyalwa Karmapa, Wangchuk Dorje (1555-1603) was heard reciting mantras in the womb. He sat cross-legged for three days soon after birth and declared he was the Karmapa. He was soon recognised by the Tai Situpa, who was staying relatively close by, and a year later by the Shamarpa who enthroned him at the age of six. Much of his life was spent in a travelling monastic camp, in which strict emphasis was placed on meditation practice. His itinerant party received invitations to visit many places. They were unable to visit China, but made important trips to Mongolia and Bhutan. Wangchuk Dorje gave many teachings in southern Tibet and restored monasteries and temples wherever he went. He also received an invitation to visit Sikkim. Unable to go himself, he sent a senior representative who established three monasteries there. The Karmapa blessed and consecrated them from Tibet. One of them was Rumtek, the present seat of the Karmapas in India.

Karmapa Wangchuk Dorje was not a prolific author but several of his texts, such as *Mahamudra, Ocean of Certain Beneficial Meaning* and *Mahamudra Dispelling the Darkness of Ignorance*, have made an important impact on the teaching of mahamudra. He and the next three Karmapas all played the role of peacemaker during the troubled political times in which they lived.

The 10th Gyalwa Karmapa, Chöying Dorje (1604-1674) took seven steps in each of the cardinal directions at birth. By the age of six, he could paint better than any of his teachers and was a gifted sculptor. Chöying Dorje foresaw the wars and political strife that were soon to come as a result of the Gelugpa-Mongol pact against the King of Tsang, whose family, followers of the Kagyu lineage, ruled most of Tibet. Thus, the 10th Karmapa distributed his wealth among the poor and needy and made Gyaltsab Rinpoche his regent, knowing he would be absent for a long time. There was much bloodshed as Gushri Khan's Mongol armies attacked first Shigatse and then the Karmapa's own camp, wreaking havoc and death. His followers saw Chöying Dorje flying off through space, holding the hand of his chief attendant. They 'landed' in the forests of Bhutan and spent more than three years living wild, helped by animals. They eventually went to what is today northern Yunnan, where the local monarch received them joyously. Altogether the 10th Karmapa spent some thirty years in exile. As always, wherever he went, he fostered the dharma and recognised incarnations of Kagyu tulkus.

The 11th Gyalwa Karmapa, Yeshe Dorje (1676-1702) was a great visionary who performed many miracles. However, he was to be the shortest lived of the Karmapas. During his precious but brief existence, he blended together the Kagyu and Nyingma teachings. He died, leaving, as his predecessor had done, a detailed letter concerning his next incarnation.

The 12th Gyalwa Karmapa, Changchup Dorje (1703-1732) studied under many illustrious masters as a young child. He gave profound Kagyu teachings to the famous Nyingma master of Katok monastery, who in turn shared his Nyingma teachings. Changchup Dorje left troubled Tibet in order to make pilgrimage to India and Nepal, accompanied by the Situ, Shamar and Gyaltsab Rinpoches. In Nepal he was thankfully honoured by the king for stopping a raging epidemic and for making rain to end a serious drought. They continued on to India, visiting the places of Lord Buddha's birth and death. The young Situpa, who impressed Indian Buddhist scholars with his erudition, became a master of languages and went on to be one of Asia's greatest scholars of all time. Returning to Tibet, the Karmapa accepted an invitation to China, and set out for that land accompanied by the Shamarpa. However, foreseeing difficult political times ahead and realising the need to leave his body, the Karmapa sent the Tai Situ a letter with details of his next incarnation and succumbed to smallpox, as did the Shamarpa two days later.

The 13th Gyalwa Karmapa, Dundul Dorje (1733-1797) had a powerful vision as a tiny child of the wrathful protector Mahakala and told many stories of his previous lives. He was recognised at the age of four and enthroned by Gyaltsab Rinpoche. At the age of eight, he met his main guru, the great 8th Situpa Chöji Jungnay, whose long life had spanned all of the 12th Karmapa's and was to span most of the 13th's. Dundul Dorje received the Kagyu transmissions from him and also studied the Nyingma teachings very extensively. He was very fond of animals and famous for communicating with them.

At one point the famous Jokhang temple, home of the Jowo image, was threatened by rising flood waters. A prophecy from Guru Rinpoche had foreseen this and predicted that only the Karmapa could do something to stop it, as it was caused by a powerful serpentine spirit (*naga*). The Lhasa authorities requested him to come. Being unable to leave immediately, he resolved the problem by writing a special letter to the naga and invoking the compassion of Avalokitesvara. On arrival at Lhasa, the 13th Karmapa offered a white scarf (*katta*) to the Jowo image, and the arms of the statue changed position to accept it. They have been that way ever since. Dundul Dorje was also asked to consecrate a distant monastery. Unable to attend, he threw blessing grains in the air at Tsurphu at the moment of the consecration ceremony, and they were seen to shower down from the heavens hundreds of kilometres away at the monastery in question.

The 14th Gyalwa Karmapa, Tekcho Dorje (1798-1868) was born in mid-winter, yet flowers spontaneously blossomed and many rainbows appeared. The baby recited the Sanskrit alphabet. He was discovered, enthroned and later ordained by the 9th Tai Situpa.

Tekcho Dorje lived very simply and exemplified the ideal monk. He was gifted in poetry and dialectics and participated in the spirit of the times, known now as *ri mé* (non-sectarian), whereby many noted scholars showed great interest in each other's traditions and teachings. There was a particularly intense exchange between the Kagyu and Nyingma traditions, with the Karmapa passing on teachings to Kongtrul Rinpoche and Jamyang Chentse Wangpo. Tekcho Dorje himself received the Vajrakilaya tantra from the Nyingma visionary treasure-text-finder Chojur Lingpa. The ritual was subsequently introduced into the Tsurphu calendar. Chojur Lingpa had important visions of future Karmapas, up to the twenty-first. These were noted down and painted in a thangka. The 14th Karmapa's spiritual heir was the great *ri mé* master and prolific author Jamgon Kongtrul Lodro Taye.

The 15th Gyalwa Karmapa, Khachab Dorje (1871-1922) was born with the highly auspicious 'treasure-hair' growing on his brow. This is one of the 32 marks of an enlightened being and was noted on the young Sakyamuni. He grew up receiving a very thorough education from famous scholars and eventually received the Kagyu transmission from Jamgon Kongtrul Lodro Taye, who also passed on to him the essence of his hundred compositions embracing the profound teachings of all Tibetan Buddhist traditions, as well as the domains of medicine, art, linguistics and general Buddhist studies. His life was a brilliant example of the bodhisattva with an insatiable desire for learning in order to help other beings. Some years before his passing, he entrusted a prediction letter to his closest attendant.

◆ ◆ ◆

These few words are but a glimpse of the lives of one of the greatest beings ever to grace this planet. A hundred times these words written by the finest of pens would not suffice to describe the wisdom, compassion, power, peace, grace and joy of that remarkable being known as *Karmapa*.

Chapter Thirteen

The Karmapa, Enlightened Activity and Buddha Nature

A fly sitting on a computer screen can have no notion of the complex intelligence lying behind the construction of its warm, bright perch; nor of the meaning of the words and images the screen displays. Even if another being could explain it all in fly language, the fly would probably never believe a word of it. It is not difficult to empathise with the fly when, on first meeting accounts of the Karmapas, one starts to contemplate the vast timescales and cosmic arenas attributed to the activity of the Buddhas in general and to the Karmapas in particular. Such stories span the lifetimes of entire universes and portray endless worlds akin to our own in which, in one form or another, the Karmapas have manifested to help others.

There are two main conceptions of the Karmapa: the one within time and the other timeless. The first views him within a context of endless worlds, existing in parallel or in sequence, within relative time. This is a little like an actor appearing in various programmes on different TV channels over a period of years. They depict a bodhisattva, almost at the end of his age-long task of purification, who has emanated thousands of times in various worlds, helping beings and working towards enlightenment, and who will eventually become the Lion Buddha, the sixth Buddha of our age. A sample story from this vast mahayana view of the bodhisattva's progress will be given in Chapter 14.

The second way of conceiving of the Karmapa, and of relating to any accomplished vajrayana master, especially the Karmapa, is in terms of the timeless play of universal purity. It is that aspect which we shall consider in this chapter.

In the greatest timescale of all, and in the deepest of senses, the Karmapa is the enlightenment at the heart of each and every one of us, known as *buddha nature*. Like a priceless diamond covered in mud, buddha nature is the fundamental purity which is the timeless true nature of mind. Although eternally present, it is constantly obscured by the superficial intensity of our worldliness. While the mud of thoughts and feelings covers a such a diamond, it cannot sparkle, it cannot shine. We might never even know that the most brilliant and resilient of jewels even exists. Yet once some mud is removed and we see the first dazzling twinkle, a road to future fortune lies open.

Although the gem of enlightenment is present, it is so deeply buried under the mud of habit that, for most people, it is imperceptible. For most of us it is no more than a theoretical potential for enlightenment. But when, either through the grace of good karma or through the effort of meditation, the mind relaxes sufficiently for something of that inner nature to shine through, it can be a very powerful experience. The appearance of holy beings in our lives often corresponds to such a time of inner awakening. This happens naturally, as the same forces of karma and interdependence are at work both within us and in the outer world.

So meeting extraordinary beings such as the Karmapa often takes place at a key moment in our spiritual life, not simply because of who the Karmapa is but because, through the power of interdependence, this necessarily happens at a time when we are closest to our Buddha potential. Although the presence of the Karmapa or great gurus can catalyse our inner potential — helping the diamond to shine for a while — it cannot do the cleaning work, the removing of the mud. We can only do that ourselves.

The time of meeting wise teachers could be thought of as the point of fruition of some good investment of the past . With new wealth in hand, we can reinvest wisely for the future — or else just fritter it away. To help in appreciating such moments and making the most of them, it can be very useful to know a little more about buddha nature and how traditionally Indians and Tibetans have approached being in the presence of holy beings. This is what the rest of this chapter will discuss.

◆ ◆ ◆

In the last decade of his life, the Buddha presented the third and final phase of his teachings — those explaining *buddha nature*. In the first phase he had taught about worldly happiness and pain and how they depend upon the way one defines oneself. He taught their counterpart: total liberation from a worldly mind through understanding the voidness of ego-projections. The second phase of his teachings presented the full extent of voidness by revealing a deeper understanding of the way the mind formulates its images not just of oneself but of the entire universe. Through this he showed not only how every experience is totally illusory but also how the way to attain enlightenment is by relating to one's own and everyone else's illusions with tremendous compassion.

Having many followers who had explored these first two phases of his teachings and who were mature enough, in every sense, to take a final step, he then taught about buddha nature. He explained that the purity, wisdom and power he himself had fully awakened through enlightenment was not unique to him but, in reality, the heart nature of each and every one of us; the indestructible diamond that lies concealed beneath the transient mud of our confusion.

In general, showing this final step was very similar to the giving of the samadhirajasutra, mentioned in an earlier chapter. It was a time to reveal the main purpose of all his teachings — a purpose that could not have been taught from the outset because his disciples' minds were not yet ready. This step-by-step approach is rather like getting someone to see clearly a specific view from a window. First you have to ask them to move left a bit, then forward a bit, and then — and only then — can they see something they could never have perceived from their original position, no matter how hard they squinted. However intelligent we are, it sometimes takes several fundamental psychological shifts, brought about by living experience, before we can see the truth.

Needless to say, this thumbnail sketch of the three phases of teaching, called the *three turnings of the wheel of dharma*, is very simplistic. The reader may remember Kalu Rinpoche's analogy of the saucer, teacup and tea, used in Chapter 4, and recognise some correspondence between the above and the three levels of Buddhist practice (hinayana, mahayana and vajrayana) to which it referred. Although it is true that there are some similarities, these are nevertheless two quite distinct topics. In the three turnings of the wheel of dharma, we are concerned with the way the Buddha introduced his disciples, through three progressive steps, to the vision of truth that he himself had discovered. It is very much to do with *philosophy* in its broadest sense as the way we each envision reality, rather than the limited sense of the domain of academic reason, whereas the three yana of the teacup analogy are to do with actual Buddhist *practice* and each person's abilities and preferences in regard to this. Yana means capacity to accomplish.

Historically, the first phase did give rise to hinayana Buddhism, which is very much founded in that view of things. The second and third phases gave rise to various schools of mahayana Buddhism, founded in the more advanced views of those phases. But vajrayana Buddhism does not have its own 'view'. Its views are those of mahayana. It is only different in the *techniques* it employs.

Let us explore the three *turnings* a little more fully. In the first phase of his teachings, the Buddha provided antidotes to people's deeply-engrained tendencies to make themselves and those around them suffer unnecessarily. His followers started to understand the cause-and-effect mechanisms at play in their minds and in life in general. They came to distinguish clearly two streams of causality leading in totally opposite directions: the one to worldly bondage and the other to liberation. These two contrary streams, each composed of causes and their effects, lie at the very heart of the Four Noble Truths[1] — the main teachings of the first turning of the wheel of dharma.

Through these teachings, the Buddha's disciples set to work on changing the various bits and pieces making up their own mentalities, using the tools of meditation, non-violence, a deep commitment to maintaining a high ethical code and so forth. Those who managed to carry their practice through to its end became *Arhats*. That meant that their mind was totally free from suffering, forever.

These first and most important teachings were given in a way that dealt with

---

[1] The Truth of Suffering (effect) describes the various realities that emerge from mistakes, described in the Truth of Origination of Suffering (cause). The Truth of Cessation of Suffering (effect) describes the peace and happiness that results from correcting those mistakes through skilful handling of one's life, described through the Truth of the Path (cause).

life and the human mind as they seem to be: real. It is inevitable — and it happens all the time today with Buddhist meditators and others undergoing an organised psychological change — that by taking the lid off the mystery of mind, the normal illusions are disempowered and the underlying structures of that mind become a central focus of attention in their own right. Anger, jealousy, personal needs, pride, love, sincerity, peace, concentration — whatever colours of the immense spectrum of mind manifest on the screen of meditation and mindfulness — become the stock-in-trade of a new reality.

One pierces the myth of one reality by understanding its infrastructure and that infrastructure subsequently becomes the new reality. For instance, to help them in their practice of understanding their inner drives, many early Buddhists kept little reserves of black and white stones next to them as they meditated, adding a white stone to a pile if they spotted a good thought and a black stone for a bad thought. In that way, they became more and more familiar with their thought processes and could evaluate their progress, or lack of it, as time went by. Penetrating deeper and deeper into the processes of the human psyche, they became able to change that psyche with ever greater efficiency.

In the West, we spoke first of alchemical compounds, then of elements, then of atoms, then of particles, then of sub-particles and so on. With each step down through the infrastructure of reality, a new and greater ability to both understand and change that reality emerges. The secret of the great lies in the small. Through understanding the atom, nuclear power was discovered. By understanding microgenetics, one can change whole animals. By understanding the tiniest of particles in a particle accelerator, the origins of the entire universe are unveiled. By meditating with ever-increasing precision, the whole nature of mind's activity becomes clear. The refinement of the whole mind, by exact understanding of its detail, was very much the focus of the Buddha's first disciples.

Although they were successfully taking apart the mechanisms of suffering, those following the first phase of the teachings were still relating to suffering and liberation as very real phenomena. They could be compared to children deeply engrossed in a film, who had finally pieced together the plot but were still so caught up in the action that they were completely unaware of being in a cinema.

This having been said, one must not underestimate the value of the Buddha's first teachings. On the contrary, they wrought an unparalleled good. But even a high mountain is low when viewed from a satellite. What the Buddha's disciples achieved in that first phase were great qualities when viewed from a worldly vantage point. Only from an absolute perspective were they not yet quite perfect.

The second phase of the Buddha's teachings provided the antidote to the side-effects caused by the first antidote. Having got to the end of the movie, the children at the cinema now looked back at the projector and realised where all that absorbing action came from. The Buddha awakened his disciples to the fact that happiness and suffering, heaven or hell, bondage or liberation or any fabrication whatsoever of the mind is simply that: no more than a fabrication of the mind. Like a dream to a dreamer, it seems totally real, enveloping and all-pervading. Like a mirage it seems to have its own existence, independent of whether one perceives it or not. But in the end, all mind states are de*void* of a lasting, independent reality of their own. This is the real implication of the word *void*ness, which has little or nothing to do with empty cosmic blue space.

This teaching was dynamite, capable of exploding many illusions. The Buddha taught it exquisitely, showing how the de-structuring of illusion needs to be founded uncompromisingly in the deepest and noblest form of compassion for oneself and others. This marriage of wisdom and compassion is of vital importance to mahayana Buddhism — the name generally given to this second phase of teaching. In this sense, compassion is not a wishy-washy sentiment but a skilful blend of five main factors, known as the five paramita. The first is great openness, a willingness to let go, to not cling to anything but on the contrary to invest everything one has in a universal good. The second is to harmonise all of one's actions into a behaviour founded in the highest ethics, modelled on the Buddha's own example. The third is to be able to cope with anyone and anything without frustration or anger; on the contrary, everything becomes an opportunity for greater courage and kindness. The fourth is to place all action within a long-term perspective, the purpose of which stretches from now until enlightenment. This big view brings a joyousness which fires diligence with enthusiasm. The fifth is to train one's mind through meditation. These five together are known as *skilful means*. The sixth paramita, famous throughout Buddhism as the prajnaparamita, is wisdom of voidness itself.

Through the careful blending of wisdom and skilful means — voidness and compassion by another name — the Buddha's entourage had made a second shift of position, and now little was needed for their view of things to be absolutely perfect. Having freed their minds from habits of suffering and having dispelled illusions about the nature of perception, the Buddha now taught the full potential of mind through a series of teachings which have since been excellently resuméd by Asanga in his fourth-century work inspired by Maitreya — the mahayanottaratantrasastra. My wife and I had the honour of being requested by His Holiness the 16th Gyalwa Karmapa to translate this text into English, which we did according to the guidance of the two teaching abbots of Rumtek at the time: Khenchen Thrangu Rinpoche and Khempo Tsultrim Gyamtso Rinpoche. It is called *Changeless Nature*.

In that extraordinary work we discover buddha nature facet by facet. It is as though the jewel in our analogy had been cleaned of mud, highly polished and then slowly examined, facet by facet, under the magnifying glass. Although it is impossible to summarise the meaning of that text — it is already a condensed summary in itself — one can say very simply that each and every one of us has the full potential of buddhahood as the very essence of our being. It is our true identity. By relating skilfully to that eternal identity, the power of spiritual awakening is triggered and a wellspring of goodness is tapped. When that happens, the 'inner' changes magnetise what happens in the 'outer' world and we meet special people. At the most powerful moments we find ourselves in the presence of Buddhas, who manifest in many ways.

This process happens the other way around, too. Sometimes it is through meeting exceptional beings that an awareness of one's enlightenment potential is activated. Gampopa gives this as one of the two great conditions for spiritual awakening, the other being a natural inclination within oneself as a result of actions in past lives.

This is why the Karmapa belongs, in the deepest sense, to this eternal timescale, the never-ending story of people awakening to their inner birthright. If we think of the Karmapa as the play of buddha-mind within personal experience — which is what his name signifies — then he is none other than that. If we relate to him from that point of view, everything he says or does proves potently pertinent to our own life and questions. One lady I met, whose faith was strong, came out of a group interview with His Holiness the 16th Karmapa, absolutely amazed that he had not only answered just the question she had on her mind, but had not asked, but also that he had answered it in Italian! Yet other people in the group had only heard him speak Tibetan and talk about things quite other. Likewise, there are also many stories of the Karmapas making statements which seemed strange at the time but which somehow engraved themselves in the listener's memory, to prove absolutely accurate a few days, or a few years, later. It is not for nothing that the Karmapa is called 'The Knower of the Past, Present and Future'. It is as though time stands still and one's whole history and future is clear to him.

The guru, and in particular the Karmapa, as the external mirror of our own buddha nature is a vital factor in vajrayana Buddhism. It means that the meeting and interaction between disciple and teacher is really the dialogue between confusion and clarity; not just a verbal dialogue but also one of body language and use of mind. The teacher's presence is a constant reminder of many things — our own life's potential, mindfulness, compassion, sense of humour, sense of seriousness — the list is as long as there are things to learn.

The fact of the Karmapa being the outer manifestation of our buddha nature is particularly true during the Vajra Crown ceremony, in which the Karmapa solemnly dons the crown offered to his fifth incarnation by the Emperor of China, who had it made to reproduce the bodhisattva crown of light he had himself seen on the Karmapa's head. It is a moment of sublime opportunity, which his disciples are convinced will keep them close to him for lives to come so that they will find the possibility of getting in touch with that buddha nature. It is also true of the moments of transmission that take place during empowerment. Something happens in those few moments that is worth many years of other sorts of spiritual practice.

One thing about the actions of enlightened beings which is often misunderstood is the fact that they do not necessarily need to plan out what they say or do to their disciples. The *Changeless Nature* makes it clear that the main qualities of buddha nature are its perfect spontaneity and absence of conceptualisation. It is perhaps also why the first and foremost of the five aspects of enlightened wisdom is known as mirror-like wisdom. Compare the simple efficiency of a mirror, as it faithfully reflects everyone and everything that comes before it, with the technology of artificial intelligence necessary to produce the same reflection using cameras, computers and TV screens.

By its very nature, enlightenment responds simply yet perfectly to each being's needs and this spontaneity, as opposed to clever thought, is the grace of the Karmapa's action. He is fearless and will not fit into other people's preconceptions of what he ought to be or ought to do. He might well place his hands tenderly and caringly on one person's head in blessing and give the next person a hearty blow if that is just what is needed. A few devoted lamas who have done a great deal for the Buddha's teachings have experienced this supreme of blessings. Who else will dare do something which mirrors to these lamas the traces of pride or self-satisfaction that still remain, and that no one else sees? It is not that the Karmapa has been planning that blow, or keeps a little notebook of who needs what done to them. It is the refreshing play of spontaneity.

Gampopa was a highly-enlightened being, a bodhisattva on the tenth level. On his way to meet Milarepa for the first time, he was told by a person who invited him to take refreshment that Milarepa had declared that his foremost disciple was now coming to him and it was clear that Gampopa was that disciple. The tiny remnants of pride left in Gampopa's being welled up in joyous happiness at this news. But on Gampopa's arrival Milarepa made him wait in a cave for a fortnight before seeing him. Who else could treat the great being predicted by the Buddha in such a way? Who else had the clarity of mind to detect the faint pride in a traveller some miles away?

These examples and stories are not chosen to frighten those about to meet the Karmapa, to most of whom he will be the radiance of loving kindness they expect of a living Buddha. They are simply a warning that he does not fit into any simplistic stereotype of the holy man and they may help one or two readers should it happen that what he says or does is very unexpected. Skill in discipleship lies in understanding how to interpret the actions of a spiritual master, knowing that one is standing before the mirror of the eternal, a mirror in which all reflections are meaningful.

Chapter Fourteen

Karmapas Long Before and Long After
the Karmapas

For cosmic aeons innumerable have I followed the unmistaken way
Of the Buddhas and Bodhisattvas of past, present and future days.
With pure, unspoilt intention from this wondrous ocean of deeds did I take
But a few drops which I crystallised these words to make.

From the 15th Karmapa's own dedication to his autobiographies
of previous ages told in 'Stainless Moonbeams'

Besides viewing the Karmapa as the outer manifestation of one's inner buddha nature, one can also consider him as the specific bodhisattva who will be the future Buddha known as Simha — 'Lion'. In this, we are helped by accounts of the bodhisattva's past emanations related by the Karmapas themselves. In the spring of 1980, the 16th Gyalwa Karmapa suggested that my wife Katia translate two works of these pre-Karmapa biographies. The first was one of his own re-collections, brought about spontaneously when, whilst travelling in Northwest India, he passed by a place where some thousand years before he had been born as a prince called Dzalendara[1], after whom the present-day city of Jullundur is named. He took birth there to help put an end to the local custom of making animal sacrifices. The introduction to the story reads:

"When His Holiness the 16th Karmapa was eight years old, he told many a story of His previous lives to one of His Gurus, Gongkar Pandita, who carefully kept in writing the nectar of the young Karmapa's words. However, when His Holiness had to leave Tibet, Gongkar Pandita was himself unable to escape and thus his precious records become unavailable. In 1976, His Holiness visited Nepal to make offerings to the three great Stupas and to bestow the empowerment (wang) and the ritual reading authorising practice (lung) of the Kagyu Nag Dzo to many of His followers. His Holiness then left Nepal for Delhi and, on the way, his party drove through a place in Himachal Pradesh called Dzalendara. It was raining very slightly and peacocks were singing softly. His Holiness had the car stopped and said to His attendants, 'I have come back to my mother-land.' He then told the following wondrous story . . ."

After the 16th Karmapa's story of Dzalendara, the book contains a collection of ten stories told by the 15th Karmapa, Khachap Dorje, about his former lives in other worlds and other times. The following is the fourth of these.

[1] In fact, it was probably something more like Jalendra, as some J sounds transliterated into Tibetan from Indian words seem to have become transformed into Dz sounds.

Prince Pure Light

> *"The very instant your pure form reflects*
> *On the myriad minds of all those various beings*
> *To be brought to spiritual maturity by the Dharma,*
> *Like on the resplendent surface of a new crystal mirror,*
> *It dispels the dust of impurity entirely.*
> *I bow down to you Chenresig, the lotus-holder."*

Ten million kalpas ago, in the age called 'The Time of Lotus Light', King 'Brilliant Sunshine of Victory' ruled the country called the 'Land of Plenty'. This country was located in the central regions of the world and was composed of 3,000 provinces, each with its local ruler. King 'Brilliant Sunshine of Victory' was the supreme monarch governing all the others. He and his seven hundred wives lived in the capital, which was an extremely beautiful town built on the banks of a majestic, slowly-flowing river. Many wild birds filled the city with their enchanting songs and the young people of the town gathered in its parks to meet and play.

Khachab Dorje took birth as the youngest of the king's sons ,'Energy of Pure Beautiful Light'. Let us call him Prince Pure Light. Prince Pure Light had a very peaceful nature and was always extremely careful and mindful in everything he did. Intelligent and well-educated, he had very good knowledge of both worldly science and religious philosophy. Practice of the ten Virtues was part of his country's law and this was highly favoured by the Prince. The people hoped dearly that it would be he who would succeed the King.

One fine morning, when the birds were singing even more sweetly than usual and the flowers filled the air with their subtle incense, the Prince and some of his companions went for a stroll in one of the parks in the southern quarter of the city. They were enjoying the exquisite beauty of the day and of their surroundings when, in a brief instant and without any warning, the sky turned black with thick clouds, a strong gale started howling and the birds flew off hurriedly to their nests. The delightful peace and beauty of the park, the enchanting sweetness of the birdsong, the relaxed ambience of the young men's enjoyment all vanished in an instant, shattered by a violent hailstorm. The change was so sudden, the contrast so vivid that the Prince realised in the instant the impermanence of all conditioned phenomena. He saw how things that are here one moment are gone the next. He felt the utter vanity and futility of his royal life and decided to devote all his efforts to the one worthwhile task — that of achieving Buddhahood, the only state beyond all changes and sorrows.

Filled with a great sadness, Prince Pure Light returned to the palace. Traces of tears on his downcast face betrayed his inner feelings and his father asked him why he looked so unhappy. The Prince realised that if he told the truth, his father would prevent him from realising his wish to become a monk and that he would be forever tied to his royal duties. Thus he told a 'white lie', saying that he really felt well and happy but that dust from the road had irritated his eyes and made him cry. However, that night, when the Prince retired to bed, he realised that the next day he would once again be confronted with the impossibility of embracing the religious life and that having fooled his father this once was of little help.The Prince prayed with deep longing,

"Buddhas, Bodhisattvas, gods and nagas, Please look upon me with compassion, Free me from the prison of royalty. Help me, since I am unable to help myself."

Praying fervently in this way, he eventually fell asleep. In the middle of the night he dreamt that Indra spoke to him from the midst of the heavens, saying: "Pure Light, tell me what is worrying you so and I will try to help you."

The Prince replied, "I want to lead a meaningful life. I realise that the vicious circle of conditioned existence is like a pit of fire and I, unfortunately, am chained to it by the shackles of karma and negativity and I cannot free myself. You have the ability to work miracles, so please, please, help me break loose from my bonds and lead me to a good Mahayana teacher."

The god replied: "I will take you to the Grove of 'Great Beauty and Felicity' where there dwells the Bodhisattva 'Freedom from the World'. He is exactly the kind of teacher you long to meet." Having said this, Indra flew away into the sky and, still dreaming, the young Prince flew after him.

He awoke to find himself surrounded by a sky that the dawn was painting pink. He was on top of a very high mountain — far, far away from his home. Looking towards the pastel dawn sky and the newly rising sun, he saw a vast plain. In the middle of the plain he saw all sorts of luxuriant trees, rich greenery and attractively-shaped rocks. He knew immediately that he must be looking at the 'Grove of Great Beauty and Felicity' that Indra had spoken of in his dream. He went directly to the grove and there he found the Bodhisattva giving teachings to a large assembly of people and gods. The Prince wished he had an offering to present to the Bodhisattva, but he had nothing with him, so he gently, carefully, picked some of the beautiful wild flowers which covered the ground like a pastel carpet and, with his heart full of pure intention, offered them to his teacher, tossing them in the sky. The flowers fell to the ground like raindrops and an unusual, delicious fragrance filled the whole place.

The teacher asked the Prince who he was, from where he had come and whether his journey had been tiring.

The Prince replied: "I come from 'The Land of Plenty', to the north of here, where my father, King Brilliant Sunshine, is ruler. I am his third and youngest son, Prince Pure Light, but I no longer wish to be involved with the royal life. I have seen the vanity of the round of conditioned existence, where everything is impermanent and breeds suffering and I truly wish to be able to help those who are immersed in this suffering to escape from it. This is why I have come to you, in the hope that you will give me a teaching able to fulfil my aspirations."

The teacher replied: "You are truly one who already long, long ago has resolved to reach Enlightenment for the benefit of all beings. Therefore, you should now take Monastic Ordination and the Bodhisattva Vow and work in this life for the good of other beings to the best of your ability."

Filled with joy and gratitude, the Prince took the Ordination and Bodhisattva Vow from his teacher. When he was given his new name, 'Intelligence of Dharma', it echoed three times through space.

His teacher then told him: "Now you should go to a place about 800 kilometres from here because there is a being there you are meant to help through your compassion."

Full of joy, 'Intelligence of Dharma' went to fulfil his duty of compassion. One day, as he was walking through a very dense forest, he met a tigress accompanied by two cubs. They were hungry, trying to find something to eat. 'Intelligence of Dharma' understood that he had reached the goal of his journey and with great joy and overwhelming compassion he opened his veins and let his blood pour into the tigress's mouth. He then gave her his body to devour and passed away, uniting his mind with that of Chenresig, the compassion aspect of total enlightenment.

This was the Fourth Story wherein Khahab Dorje,
as the son of King Brilliant Sunshine,
offered his body to a tigress.

Saraha

The three points about a Karmapa which may spring to a Tibetan lama's mind are that he is an emanation of Avalokitesvara, he is the reincarnation of Saraha and he will be the 6th Buddha of the Age: Buddha Simha. In the chapter on the Vajra Crown, we will see how he is considered to be Avalokitesvara.

Saraha was one of the greatest of India's 84 mahasiddhas. *Maha* means great and *Siddhi* means accomplishment, of which there are two main types: general and supreme. To achieve mastery over the primary elements of existence and perform extraordinary things through the power of mind is to attain general siddhi. To become the ultimate perfection of mind is to attain ultimate siddhi. Some of the 84 mahasiddhas had achieved the former and some the latter.

The 3rd Karmapa, Rangjung Dorje, puts the birth of Saraha 336 years after Lord Buddha's passing, i.e. 210 BCE. He was known as the 'Great Brahmin' because as a child in southern India he was one of five erudite Brahmin brothers. He became a Buddhist monk, receiving the name Rahula, and went on to become a famous Buddhist scholar, but still known as the 'Brahmin Rahula', one of the teachers of Nagarjuna. One day he met his guru Sukhanatha who sent him to a dakini who was an arrowsmith. Using symbolic teachings, she enlightened him, showing him meanings through the acts of arrow-making and archery. Through this he became known as Saraha(n) — he who has shot the arrow.

His vajrayana practices and association with a woman of lower caste than his provoked criticism and vilification from the Brahmin community and eventually from the local royal family. In response to this he sang mystical songs (*doha*), first to the people, then to the queen and finally to the king himself, eventually leading them all to liberation. The doha addressed to the people, the queen and the king are a great treasury of most profound instruction. These teachings were handed down in living lineage through to the beginning of the Kagyu tradition, a millennium later, and have been preserved until the present day. From him come the fully-detailed meditation teachings of *mahamudra*, on the nature of mind, and how to attain that through skilful meditations working directly with mind itself, rather than through techniques using the skilful imagery and channelling of the various tantras. He himself received those teachings from the celestial bodhisattva Great Jewel of Intelligence and transmitted them to the illustrious Nagarjuna. Nagarjuna in turn passed them to his disciple Shawari who transmitted them to Maitripa., who was Marpa's guru. Thus Marpa received the mahamudra transmission from two sources, Naropa and Maitripa, the former using the skilful means of yoga and the latter working directly with the processes of awareness, perception and consciousness.

Simha — the Lion Buddha

According to the Buddhist scriptures, our world is a very fortunate one. Although endless cosmic systems exist, many of them inhabited, ours is graced by the advent of 1002 Buddhas during its existence. Each of them teaches the dharma fully. Sakyamuni, the Buddha of our age, was but the fourth of these and is special inasmuch as he came at a time which is 'darker' than any of the more golden ages in which the other Buddhas come. For this reason, he is the only one of them to teach vajrayana: the powerful technique needed to combat the powerful passions and defilements typical of the times in which his teaching has effect.

It is said that his teachings will last in all some 5,000 years and that there will then follow a time of decline, in which the life and the physical and mental qualities of this planet's inhabitants will deteriorate, while simultaneously the quality of the environment and its power to nourish and bring pleasure will also decline. At its worst, the average human lifespan will be of the order of just ten years. During this sombre and decadent time, the bodhisattva Maitreya will manifest, so beautiful and self-composed that people, wishing to be like him, will heed his teachings on causality. He will spend many lives gathering beings to him and gradually the practice of virtue will be restored. Consequently the lifespan and the quality of life will improve until it far exceeds that of our present times. He will then emanate in his final bodhisattva existence in which he becomes Buddha

Maitreya (Maitri means loving kindness).

As the ages pass, it will then be time for the bodhisattva who is presently known to us as the Karmapa to appear. Beings who have a link with him, be it positive or negative, will gather to him throughout his bodhisattva lives. Those with a negative link, forged through bad karma, will gradually purify their mistakes and make positive connections. Those who already have positive links will strengthen them. The growth in virtue and understanding will develop, life after life, and the momentum of forthcoming enlightenment will draw to it all those destined to be disciples of the 6th Buddha, the Lion. By that time, it is predicted that beings will be much, much more subtle in body and mind than at present, with extraordinarily long lifespans by our standards. Then will come the existence in which he attains enlightenment in the eyes of the world. At that time, all those connected to him will find themselves in the Buddha's true presence at the moment when the timeless teachings are once again imparted to the world. With this longer-term perspective in mind and a deeply compassionate wish to help all beings, Kagyu followers believe that any connection that someone makes with the Karmapa will sow a seed that can gradually come to its fruition, at least by the time of the 6th Buddha, if not sooner. The *Good Age Sutra* says that

> *Buddha Simha will be born into a royal family in a city with a name meaning 'Flower God'. His light aura will be of one paktse (several kilometres) in size. His father's name will mean 'Lion Tiger' and his mother's 'Roar of Joy'. He will have a son known as 'Great Might'. His main attendant will be called 'Peaceful', his wisest follower 'Burning Wisdom' and the most miraculously-endowed follower 'Cloud-endowed'. In a first wave of dharma he will teach a thousand million beings, in a second wave nine hundred million and in a third wave some eight hundred million. His life will endure seventy thousand years and his teachings will endure for a million years. His relics will be distributed in various places.*

Chapter Fifteen

The Vajra Crown and the
All-Liberating Karmapa Black Pills

The origin of the Karmapa Vajra Crown goes back to very ancient times, when the bodhisattva Avalokitesvara emanated in human form as the son of King Yungkhorsung somewhere in central Asia. His life was the very epitome of enlightened compassion towards all beings. On a universal level, Avalokitesvara is the form taken by the enlightened ultimate essence of mind as it radiates its help towards every relative state of mind. Avalokitesvara is very special to the land of Tibet, where he is known as Chenresig — 'The All-Seeing'. After years of solitary meditation in remote mountains, this emanation of Avalokitesvara attained the greatest of accomplishments (*siddhi*) and vast assemblies of buddhas and bodhisattvas gathered to honour him. They presented him with a crown said to be 'woven from the hair of one hundred thousand celestial beings'.

This seems to be the repetition, relatively within our age, of a similar event described in the Lankaravatara Sutra. Ananda, Lord Buddha's chief attendant, asks the Buddha about the Vajra Crown. The Buddha tells him how, a long time past, in a world where beings had transcendent bodies and lived for exceptionally long periods, in an age long before that of the previous Buddha Dipankara, a prince called Dharma Intelligence meditated for a hundred million years on a mountainside. The dakini came from all directions to honour his depth and extent of samadhi. Thirteen million dakini came, each offering a strand of their hair, from which they wove the Vajra Crown. They then ornamented it with divine jewels.

This worthy emanation continued to reincarnate, appearing in our times in India in many forms and particularly in one very famous emanation as the great mahasiddha Saraha and another as Padmasambhava. Other emanations include the great scholars Asvagosa and Nagabhodi and the dharma king Indrabhuti. Subsequently this line of emanations of Avalokitesvara appeared in Tibet as Dusum Khyenpa, the first Karmapa, and since then as the various Karmapas. All of them have been seen by those with pure minds as wearing the celestial crown, yet it is usually invisible to the human eye. When the young 16th Karmapa went to HH the 13th Dalai Lama, who was to perform the 'hair-cutting' and naming ceremony, he was wearing a small fabric crown, yet the Dalai Lama saw him as wearing another on top of it. The Karmapa removed the small crown and made prostration. The Dalai Lama enquired why he had not removed the other crown and was told by his attendant that the Karmapa was definitely bare-headed. They then realised that the pure vision of the Dalai Lama had allowed him to see the normally invisible celestial crown.

The fifth Karmapa, Deshin Shekpa, was the guru of the Chinese emperor Yung-Lo (Ch'eng Tsu), himself a bodhisattva. The latter had seen the celestial crown and requested permission of the Karmapa to make a replica of it, so that all beings could have the blessing of seeing it. When he offered the completed crown to the Karmapa, he prayed that it should be blessed with the power of liberating beings from the sufferings of the world. In the Lankaravatara sutra, it predicts:

> *The one wearing the vajra crown along with the monastic robes*
> *will ceaselessly benefit beings until the very time*
> *when the teaching of the thousand buddhas comes to its end.*

Furthermore, Padmasambhava predicted:

> *An emanation of Avalokitesvara's speech emanated from the Tusita Heaven for the benefit of all beings. The first incarnation, known as Dusum Chenpa, the one of mantrayana activity, bears the black crown as a mark of empowerment and as the head adornment of his group. Each moment of his life, he guides limitless beings to enlightenment. Anyone who sees, hears, recollects or has contact with these Karmapas will, on leaving this life, be reborn before Avalokitesvara.*

The crown offered by Emperor Ch'eng Tsu is known as the *U-sha tong drol chenmo*. The 10th Karmapa spent some thirty years in exile in Jang (present-day Yunnan). During that time, the Emperor of Jang had an exact replica of the Ch'eng Tsu crown made. This is known as the *Jang sha*. Since the replica crown was offered, the Karmapas have performed the Vajra Crown ceremony as an important part of their enlightened activity. Traditionally, the *U-sha tong drol chenmo* was always kept at Tsurphu and the *Jang sha* was taken on trips away. The Karmapa used whichever crown accordingly. No one knows which of the two the 16th Karmapa took with him when he left Tibet in 1959. The one which remained was slightly abused and damaged by the Chinese army and has since been kept in the Potala palace.

In the Vajra Crown ceremony, the Karmapa, wearing another form of headgear, often the meditation hat of Gampopa, seats himself upon an elevated throne which all can see. His monks chant, on behalf of those attending the ceremony, a request for him to assume his transcendent form of Avalokitesvara and call upon the patriarchs of the Kagyu lineage for blessing.

A rice mandala, symbolic of everything good in the universe, is created on a plate of precious metal and offered to His Holiness. Then the traditional Buddhist seven-part prayer is chanted:

1. homage and prostration to the Gyalwa Karmapa as Avalokitesvara
2. physical, verbal and mental offerings are made
3. former mistakes and impurities are regretted and purified
4. the enlightened activity of Avalokitesvara is praised
5. the Karmapa as Avalokitesvara is requested to turn the wheel of dharma for all beings

HH the 16th Karmapa performing the Vajra Crown ceremony

6. he is requested to remain in the world to help beings and
7. the goodness of these six acts is dedicated to the welfare of all beings.

The point of the seven-part practice is to create an intense moment of positive karma and to set the mind in the correct frame of openness and receptivity. In response, the Karmapa removes the Gampopa crown and, reciting the OM MANI PADME HUNG mantra of Avalokitesvara on a crystal rosary, lets manifest the radiant compassion of enlightenment which is, in verity, his constant heart-essence. During this time, in as best a state of meditative calm, devotion and mindfulness as they can manage, the audience prepares itself. The Karmapa then dons the Vajra Crown and there occurs as much transmission of blessing as can be received by each member of the assembly, according to his or her openness. The

The 12th Tai Situpa places the small bodhisattva crown on the head of the 17th Karmapa,
Urgyen Trinley Dorje

ceremony concludes with dedication prayers chanted by the monks and, depending on the circumstances, a personal blessing for those present as they chant together the MANI mantra. The sponsors of the ceremony receive special blessing threads and dharma medicines, prepared from relics, among which are the famous Karmapa black pills.

Karmapa black pills

One important aspect of the Karmapa's enlightened activity is to make and bless a very special substance, given in the form of small black pills, called *ril nak*. They are believed to bring extraordinary blessing, through the power of interdependence, from the Karmapa to the people who wear them or, in the face of dangerous circumstances, eat them. They are usually carried as a blessing and protection, often in a relic box worn around the neck or on the body. If ingested at the time of death, they are believed to aid liberation, by the power of connection with the Karmapa, causing one to meet him in the form of Avalokitesvara and be guided by him to a better condition. The pills are rare and it is considered highly fortunate to have the chance to take one before dying.

The pills are also a support in sickness. In a case of serious illness, they may bring a physical improvement or remission that seems impossible. Modern doctors in communist China have been nonplussed by the results of the Karmapa

pills, which they have researched and found to be extraordinarily but inexplicably effective. There have been many cases of people very near to death gaining a year's remission, during which time many special things happen in their life, making death itself less traumatic for the patient and those left behind. The pills often remove the bitterness and depression that can afflict those with chronic serious illness, giving courage and a certain peace.

The Karmapa pills are made by His Holiness using special ingredients, some of them relics, such as a plough used by Marpa the Translator and a stone building implement used by Jetsun Milarepa. It is the latter which give the *ril nak* their black colour. His Holiness picks several lamas of pure conduct and strong spirituality to help him in the actual making of the pills. They rise early on the chosen day of fabrication, cleanse themselves and recite a special prayer known as the *guru yoga of the 8th Karmapa*. Later, while rolling the tiny (about 1mm) pills, they recite the mantra *Karmapa Chenno*. The Karmapa makes the mixture for the pills from a tsampa base, to which are added precious ingredients from the relic treasury. He rolls larger (3-4 mm) 'mother' pills himself. From the 'dough', enough pills are rolled to fill the 3rd Karmapa's begging bowl to about two thirds. At the end of the day, it is covered with the robe of the 3rd Karmapa and laid on a cloth where it remains overnight.

During the night the pills multiply, overspilling onto the surrounding cloth. Multiplication is one of the extraordinary qualities attributed to the Karmapa mother pills, sometimes even the smaller pills. One particular friend of mine, a very rational surgeon who shunned the 'miraculous' side of Buddhism, was

astounded to find that the pill he had been given and worn had turned into seven of the same size. There are many similar accounts of this happening. One lama carried a few mother pills around with him in a small case and had a constant supply of 'baby' pills to give for the very sick and dying. Some say that the pills reproduce in the presence of a virtuous mind.

At the time of writing, HH the 17th Karmapa has not travelled from his traditional seat at Tsurphu to the relatively more recently established seat at Rumtek in Sikkim, India. It is there, in the treasury, that the Vajra Crown and precious relics needed for making the Karmapa *ril nak* are stored for the present, and only the Karmapa may use them. Although the Karmapas have endless emanations of all sorts throughout the world, there is only one enthroned Gyalwa Karmapa, the presence within the Karma Kamtsang of the Buddha's enlightened activity. Although the enthroned Gyalwa Karmapa's activity accomplishes many tasks within the hinayana, mahayana and vajrayana lineages that he perpetuates, the Vajra Crown ceremony and the making of the pills are unique and traditional facets of his activity for which he has been particularly famed over the centuries. It will be a tremendous joy for Kagyu followers all over the world when Urgyen Trinley Dorje goes to Rumtek and makes contact with these holy objects so that their blessing may reach thousands of followers, bringing liberation through seeing, hearing, touching and recollection.

OM SVASTI SIDDHAM

*Wondrously-manifesting embodiment of primordial wisdom, endowed with
the magnificence of an ocean of qualities which liberate and bring beings to maturity,
crowning glory of the Buddhas of the three times, Karmapa,
may your sacred presence remain long with us and your enlightened activity spread.*

*Wondrous is your ability to manifest from the vast expanse of dharmadhatu
within the conventional reality of the world, just as is wished,
Triumphant One, master of all things in the three realms and the three times,
who can go where it is difficult to go,
may your sacred presence remain long with us and your enlightened activity spread.*

*Providing an opportunity for liberation through sight, sound, recollection or contact,
blazing with the splendour of perfect wisdom, universal love and great ability,
endowed with the light of virtue and excellence, which dispels the threefold darkness,
may your sacred presence remain long with us and your enlightened activity spread.*

*Adorning the three trainings with immense purity of right conduct, your mind, fully
mature through the three masteries and study, contemplation and meditation,
has the power to cause others' minds to be liberated;
may your sacred presence remain long with us and your enlightened activity spread.*

*Through the total purity of the various immaculate dharmas, both of
the teachings in general and those of the practice lineage in particular,
may your sacred presence remain long with us and your enlightened activity spread,
fulfilling and satisfying the hopes of all, in every single place in this vast world.*

*You teach and appear in many different ways — a veritable ocean of manifestations
of wondrous miracles, beyond estimation and beyond the imagination,
that every concept of coming, going or staying be transcended,
may your sacred presence remain long with us and your enlightened activity spread.*

*In brief, lord and protector of the world, who embraces a hundred enlightened classes of
being, glorious guru, power of the buddhas, Karmapa,
may your sacred presence remain long with us and your enlightened activity spread.
May your enlightened activity pervade to the furthest limits of every quarter.*

*Through prayer from the depths of one's being, made with faith and deep devotion,
through the compassion of an ocean of enlightened beings and of the three sources,
and through the power of truth which is the utter purity of the essence of all,
may this highly meaningful prayer be swiftly accomplished, just as is intended.*

[This long-life prayer is an adaptation of the famous one composed by the Tai Situ Pema Wang-cho Gyalpo for the 16th Gyalwa Karmapa, Rangjung Rikpe Dorje. It has been modified by Tai Situ Pema Dönyö as a prayer addressed to the 17th Gyalwa Karmapa, the all-pervading Urgyen Drodul Trinley Dorje.]

Glossary of Buddhist Terms

Asoka   India's most famous Buddhist monarch. He had stone pillars erected at important Buddhist places, to commemorate events in Lord Buddha's life.

Asanga   One of the main persons involved in the development of mahayana Buddhism. He is seen as being directly inspired by the great bodhisattva and future Buddha, Maitreya.

Avalokitesvara   The bodhisattva who is the embodiment of perfect compassion.

Bardo   This term is most popularly associated with the state in between two incarnations. It really refers to the fact that all states are 'in-between', in the impermanent nature of worldly life.

Bodhicitta   Dedication to achieving enlightenment, so as to be able to help relieve the sufferings of others.

Bodhisattva   A follower of mahayana Buddhism — someone whose life is dedicated to achieving total enlightenment, so as to be able to help relieve the sufferings of others.

Buddhahood   The highest and purest state anyone could ever achieve, it is a mind totally clear, because it is free from every trace of ignorance, and a mind that is replete with every quality of love, compassion, wisdom and power to help others.

Buddha nature   The potential for enlightenment universally present in any being. For a fuller explanation see Chapter 13 — The Karmapa, Enlightened Activity and Buddha Nature.

Cakrasamvara   A very important set of teachings belonging to the vajrayana tradition. They were introduced into Tibet by Marpa.

Chakra   This is the Sanskrit word for wheel. It is used figuratively to denote the places in the body which are centrepoints, or convergence points, of energy.

Dakini   'Celestial being' — there are various sorts, some being manifestations of enlightenment itself and others being worldly entities endowed with special powers. A fuller account can be found in Tai Situpa's *Tilopa*.

Dharmacakra   'Wheel of dharma' — dharma is the teaching of universal truth. Buddhas teach this over and over again in various worlds. The repetitive, cyclic nature of this is compared to the turning of a wheel. It contrasts with the notion of samsara — 'repetitive existence' — where the driving force is ignorance, which obscures the truth.

Doha   Song or poem used to convey the deepest teachings.

Dream yoga   Practice which develops total lucidity while dreaming and enables one to use the dream state as a tool for enlightenment.

Dzogchen   'Great Perfection' — the highest teachings of the Nyingma tradition of Tibetan Buddhism. These teachings are their equivalent of mahamudra — the Great Seal teachings of the Kagyu tradition.

Gcod   Vajrayana practice for releasing the mind from attachment and developing total generosity of being.

Gelugpa   One of the four main Tibetan traditions of Buddhism, founded in the 14th century by Tsong Khapa.

Great Seal   The literal translation of *mahamudra*, the name of the highest teachings of Buddhism and the very heart of the Kagyu lineage.

Greater way   Mahayana — a level of Buddhism rooted in total compassion and a path of practice which leads to buddhahood.

Guru Rinpoche   This name has two significances. The first is specific and refers to the historical person whose spiritual power enabled Buddhism to establish itself in Tibet in the 8th century. He was also known as Padmasambhava — 'The Lotus-Born Guru'. The second significance is universal and refers to the general ability of buddha nature to manifest as gurus and teachers, protecting and guiding beings in many worlds in many different ways.

Heat yoga   *gtum.mo* — a yogic practice which progressively purifies and masters the whole psycho-physical complex which constitutes a human being.

Illusory body yoga   A powerful practice which reveals the illusory nature of all things.

Indestructible way   *Vajrayana* — a special area of mahayana Buddhism, distinguished by its powerful techniques (see Chapter 10).

Interdependence   One of the main Buddhist teachings, which demonstrates how nothing exists in its own right but only in dependence upon other things.

Jokhang   Temple founded in Lhasa by the 7th-century Tibetan king Söntsen Gampo to house a rare and beautiful statue of the Buddha brought from China by his new bride.

Jowo   The name of the Buddha statue brought to Tibet by princess Wen-Ch'eng (see previous entry).

Kagyu   One of Tibet's four main traditions of Buddhism, brought to Tibet from India by Marpa in the late 11th century (see Chapter 11).

Kalacakra   'Wheel of Time' teachings, describing all relationships between things in the various universes, throughout time, from a vast and profound vajrayana point of view.

Karma   The Buddhist doctrine that one's actions determine one's future lot, virtuous actions leading to happiness and unvirtuous ones leading to suffering (see Chapter 7).

Karma Kagyu   The Kagyu tradition, stemming from the Indian saint Tilopa, and brought to Tibet by Marpa, had four main and eight minor lineages in Tibet. The Karma Kagyu, one of the four major traditions, is the one centred around the Karmapa incarnations. It is also known as the Karma Kamtsang.

Karma Kamtsang   See previous entry.

Madhyamika   The famous Buddhist 'Middle Way' — a philosophical stance which avoids all the extreme views of reality generated by a deluded intellect. It has nothing to do with compromising between extremes. It simply means avoiding them.

Mahamudra   See above entry on *Great Seal*.

Mahasiddha   One who has achieved very great accomplishment through meditation.

Mahayana   See above entry on *Greater Way*.

Middle Way   See above entry on *Madhyamika*.

Nadi   In tangible reality these are the channels through which the body's vitality is maintained — principally those of the central nervous system and blood vessels. In meditation it is a stylised reproduction of these, using flowers and interconnecting pathways.

Naga   A serpentine being, part god, part animal. Some of them, like the dragons of western lore, are guardians of great treasuries.

Nirmanakaya   Manifestation of the Buddha that ordinary persons with very good karma are able to experience, if the circumstances are right.

Nirvana   The end of all suffering. This term does not, as many believe, refer to a certain state. It only specifies what is no longer present — which has been transcended forever.

Panchen Lama   A very important lama of the Gelugpa tradition.

Paramita   'That which carries one to the other shore' — these are the practices which bring enlightenment. They are perfection in generosity, right conduct, forbearance, diligence, meditation and wisdom. The last of these is known as prajnaparamita. For a fuller explanation see Gampopa's *Gems of Dharma, Jewels of Freedom.*

Powa   The art of guiding consciousness, especially at the moment of death.

Potala   The name of Avalokitesvara's pure land. It is used for the palace in Lhasa which was home to the Dalai Lamas.

Prajnaparamita   See above entry on *Paramita.*

Protectors   Psychic forces which deflect the strength of evil and protect the growth of loving kindness, care and wholesomeness.

Relative truth   Truth in terms of the way things seem to be.

Root lama   The personal guru. Technically one only has a root lama once one has 'seen' the ultimate truth. It is the person who guides one to that moment of seeing.

Sambhogakaya   The way enlightenment manifests to those great bodhisattvas who have definitively penetrated the meaning of voidness.

Sangha   The Buddhist community, especially that of monks and nuns and very especially that of those who have definitively penetrated the meaning of voidness.

Subtle body   The body seen more in a dynamic, or energetic, than static anatomical way, as energy flows and as the home of transcendent reality.

Terma   Texts concealed by Guru Rinpoche in the 8th century and discovered by special lamas — *ter tön* — as and when the world needs them.

Tripitaka   The 'three collections', namely sutra, vinaya and abhidharma, containing all the recorded teachings of Lord Buddha — some one hundred volumes in all.

Tulku   Literally 'emanation' — either of the Buddha or of a great bodhisattva. The term was also applied to the reincarnations of very special lamas who had not yet reached the 'great bodhisattva' level.

Ultimate truth   Truth in terms of the way things really are.

Urgyen   The land from which Guru Rinpoche came. Some identify it as present-day Eastern Afghanistan.

Vajra   A mythical weapon, able to destroy anything, yet itself indestructible.

Vajrayana   The most powerful of all Buddhist teachings. See Chapter 10 which is dedicated to this subject.

Voidness   Wisdom which understands things to be de*void* of the independent reality they seem to have. All things depend upon other things for their existence — hence the importance in Buddhism of understanding the processes of interdependence.

Yana   A *capacity* for understanding or for practising or for coping with the different Buddhist teachings.

Yidam   An aspect of meditation which links one with certain specific qualities of ultimate reality.

Bibliography

Ancient Tibet, *Yeshe De Project,* Dharma,1986

Buddha's Lions, *Abhayadatta,* Dharma, 1979

The Changeless Nature, *Maitreya/Asanga, Tr. Holmes,* KDDL, 1985

La Civilisation Tibétaine, *Rolf Stein,* Le Sycomore — L'Asiathèque,1962

Dzalendara and Sakarchupa — stories from the fomer lives of the Gyalwa Karmapas, *HH Gyalwa Karmapa, Tr. Katia Holmes,* KDDL, 1981

Foundations of Tibetan Medicine, *Finckh,* Watkins, 1978

Gems of Dharma, Jewels of Freedom, *Jé Gampopa, Tr. Kenneth & Katia Holmes,* Altea Publishing, 1994

Gso-ba Rig-pa: la Médecine Tibétaine, *Dr F Meyer,* CNRS, Paris

Health Through Balance — an Introduction to Tibetan Medicine, *Dr Yeshi Donden,* Snow Lion, 1986

The History of the Sixteen Karmapas of Tibet, *Lama Karma Thinley,* Prajna Press, 1980

The Hundred Thousand Songs of Milarepa, *Tr. C C Chang,* Shambala,1962

Karmapa the Black Hat Lama of Tibet, *Douglas & White,* Luzac, 1976

The Life of Buddha as Legend and History, *Edward Thomas,* RKP, 1927/1975

The Life of Marpa, *Tsang Nyon Heruka,* Prajna Press, 1982

The Life of Milarepa, *Tr. L.P.Lhalungpa,* E.P.Dutton,1977

The Life of the Buddha, *Saddhatissa,* Unwin, 1976

Mahamudra, *Thrangu Rinpoche,* Snow Lion, 1995

Mahamudra: Dispelling the Darkness of Ignorance, *9th Karmapa, Wangchuk Dorje,* LTWA

Nomads of Western Tibet, *Goldstein/Bell,* Serindia

Relative World, Ultimate Mind, *Twelfth Tai Situpa,* Shambhala, 1992

The Royal Song of Saraha, *Tr. H.Guenther,* Shambhala/RKP, 1973

Tilopa (some glimpses of his life), *XIIth Khentin Tai Situpa,* Dzalendara, 1988

2500 years of Buddhism, *ed. Bapat,* Ministry of Information and Broadcasting, India, 1956.

Way to Go, *Khentin Tai Situpa,* KDDL.

Kagyu Centres

Readers who would like to obtain the addresses of Kagyu Centres in their own area should contact Samye Ling Tibetan Centre, Eskdalemuir DG13 0QL, Scotland. Tel: +44 13873 73232 / Fax: +44 13873 73223

Tsurphu Monastery, Tibet

Tsurphu Monastery, the traditional seat of the Karmapas, is situated at an altitude of 4,600 metres (14,700 ft) about a two-hour drive northwest of Lhasa, the capital of central Tibet. Its location is stunning — a narrow valley with an abundance of leafy trees (willows and poplars) in summer and meadows bordering the rushing stream below the old boundary walls. All the Karmapas without exception have lived here and this is where the 17th Karmapa resides today. From here the Karmapas extend their blessings to the world.

Although the physical structure of Tsurphu and its sacred works of art were destroyed during the Chinese Cultural Revolution, the blessings of the lineage have remained so strongly present that spiritually the site remains unblemished. Tsurphu once housed 900 monks and four major colleges. Currently, over 400 monks live and study within the walled complex.

The project to rebuild Tsurphu began in 1981 when His Holiness the 16th Karmapa asked Drupon Dechen Rinpoche, the former retreat master of Tsurphu, to return to Tibet and supervise the reconstruction. In 1983, the people of Tsurphu got permission and funds equivalent to US$5,000 from the Lhasa government to begin rebuilding and in 1984 one of the colleges was completed. In this same year, Tai Situ Rinpoche and Jamgon Kongtrul Rinpoche visited Tsurphu. At that time, the government granted permission to rebuild the entire monastery.

In 1986, the reconstruction of the original Tsurphu retreat facility ('Drubtra Samten Ling') was completed and 15 monks entered the traditional three-year retreat. Also being rebuilt is the Lhakang of Sertung, the main temple in the monastery complex with walls literally 3 metres thick, which was one of the first buildings at Tsurphu centuries ago. It will house three large Buddha images (Sakyamuni, Karma Pakshi and Guru Rinpoche) in the bottom floor of the main shrine room and on upper floors, among other facilities, will be the main residence room and reception room of HH the 17th Karmapa.

The construction of the Tsurphu Guest House ('Kunga Delek') is complete and it is open for visitors. With about forty rooms, including a kitchen and a small shrine room, it offers simple accommodation to disciples and devotees of His Holiness the 17th Karmapa.

Visiting Tsurphu is extremely worthwhile. The purity and peace of this sacred place are beyond imagination. It is a paradise for Buddhist practitioners and a source of endless inspiration and joy in these restless times in the outside world.

We are grateful to Ward Holmes for providing the above information from his Tsurphu Foundation World Wide Web pages, which contain a wealth of beautifully presented facts and photographs on Tsurphu and the 17th Karmapa, Urgyen Trinley Dorje. We highly recommend these pages to anyone contemplating a journey to Tsurphu, as many useful details for visitors are provided, or indeed to anyone who is generally interested in the subject.

Internet address: http://www.maui.net/~tsurphu/karmapa

Readers who wish to support the rebuilding of Tsurphu Monastery may send donations to:

ROKPA Trust, Samye Ling, Eskdalemuir, Dumfriesshire DG13 0QL, **Scotland**, or
Tsurphu Foundation, 1135 Makawao Ave., Suite 103-307, Makawao, Hawaii 96768, **USA**.

About the Author

Ken Holmes, born in London in 1947, left his early career in chemical engineering to manage a project helping homeless addicts in central London. On completion of this, he set out in 1969 to meet in person the Sufi and Tibetan mystics he had read about since his childhood. His travels led him through the Middle East and Afghanistan to India, where he spent six months in Dharamsala studying with the monks of HH the Dalai Lama. From there he went to Kagyu Samye Ling, the first Tibetan Buddhist centre established in the West. This has been his base for the past 25 years, during which time his life has been devoted to making Tibetan Buddhist meditation and philosophy available to the western world. He and his wife Katia have translated some of the main Kagyu teaching texts into English as well as much of the liturgy used in daily Buddhist practice.

In 1977 Ken spent six months travelling with His Holiness the 16th Karmapa as one of his assistants for his European tour. It was during this time that His Holiness encouraged him and Katia to enter into intensive study of Kagyu texts and to prepare accurate English translations based upon the traditional lineage explanations. Ken is presently Director of Studies at Kagyu Samye Ling, where he teaches, translates and interprets for visiting Tibetan lamas.

Books

Translated with Katia Holmes, from the Tibetan: *Changeless Nature* — root text, by Maitreya/Asanga; 1979, KDDL. *Dzalendara and Sakarchupa — stories from the former lives of the Karmapas*, by the 15th and 16th Karmapas; 1981, KDDL. *Changeless Nature* (expanded edition), by Maitreya/Asanga; 1985, KDDL. *Gems of Dharma, Jewels of Freedom*, by Jé Gampopa; 1994, Altea Publishing.

Edited from transcripts: *Way to Go*, by12th Tai Situpa; 1986, KDDL. *Tilopa: some glimpses of his life*, by12th Tai Situpa; 1988, KDDL. *Compassion and Understanding* (with Dr Frank Whaling), 1st Samye Symposium; 1989, KDDL.

Translation from the French: *The Art of Joyful Living*, by Drs Peze and Roche de Coppens; 1987, Element.

ROKPA Trust

Ken Holmes works for the ROKPA Trust in Scotland. ROKPA has more than forty projects in Tibet, providing education, health care, training in traditional Tibetan medicine and setting up reforestation and other schemes. It also operates in Nepal, India and other countries. For further information contact:

ROKPA Foreign Aid
Samye Ling Tibetan Centre
Eskdalemuir DG13 0QL
Scotland
Tel: +44 13873 73232
Fax: +44 13873 73223
e-mail 100645,170@compuserve.com
UK Regd. Charity No. 327395

ROKPA International
Sonnenhof 5
8121 Benglen
Switzerland
Tel: +41 1 262 6888
Fax: +41 1 262 6889

Index